KINGS OF INFINITE SPACE

Frank Lloyd Wright & Michael Graves

KINGS OF INFINITE SPACE

Frank Lloyd Wright & Michael Graves

Based on the BBC film by
CHARLES JENCKS

I could be bounded in a nutshell, and count myself a king of infinite
space, were it not that I have bad dreams.   Hamlet, II,ii,264

ACADEMY EDITIONS · LONDON/ST. MARTIN'S PRESS · NEW YORK

Also by Charles Jencks

The Language of Post-Modern Architecture (1977, 1979, revised edition 1981)
Daydream Houses of Los Angeles (1978)
Bizarre Architecture (1979)
Skyscrapers—Skycities (1980)
Late-Modern Architecture (1980)
Post-Modern Classicism (1980)
Current Architecture (1982)
Free Style Classicism (1982)
Abstract Representation (1983)

published by Academy Editions and Architectural Design, London

Front cover
Portland Public Services Building, 1980-83, detail of Madison Street elevation. The first monument to Post-Modernism. (Photo: Proto Acme Photo)

Back cover
Philip Johnson, Charles Jencks and Michael Graves in conversation in the Glass House. (Photo: Robin Lough)

Frontispiece
Michael Graves and Frank Lloyd Wright. (Photos: Robin Lough and State Historical Society of Wisconsin)

Photographs are by Charles Jencks unless otherwise credited.

First published in Great Britain in 1983 by
Academy Editions, 7 Holland Street, London W8

Published in the United States of America in 1983 by
St. Martin's Press, 175 Fifth Avenue, New York, NY10010

Library of Congress Catalogue Card Number 83-50702
ISBN 0 312 45594 1 hb ISBN 0 312 45595 x pb [USA only]

Printed and bound in Great Britain by
Eyre & Spottiswoode Ltd., London

INTRODUCTION

IN A BOOK SUCH AS THIS, BASED ON A BBC FILM OF THE SAME NAME, one is aware of taking certain risks. There is the risk, which Kenneth Clark noted, of 'literary suicide', turning the spoken into the written word, the imprecise locution into a phrase to be pondered slowly in black and white. There is also the risk of broad generalisation, a temptation and opportunity of the medium, where one must reach a broad audience with a broad message. But if these are the dangers, there is one compensating virtue: one can speculate. Here this has led to some interpretations which will no doubt be at variance with received opinion. Most unusual, I suppose, is the interpretation of Frank Lloyd Wright as a traditionalist, as the *Pre*-Modernist, not the Modern architect both he and his apologists have taken him to be. Next, in degree of controversy, is the interpretation of some of his late buildings as kitsch, but, more troublesome to standard opinion, a kitsch that is occasionally redeemable. Finally there are the interpretations of Michael Graves as Wright's logical successor, and the view of their public architecture in *private* terms. There is much here of domestic matters. But this is not psychohistory, even if it isn't purged of blood. Rather it's a new attempt to link domestic crises, sometimes very personal affairs of the heart, with changes of philosophy and style. Private and public life don't always change together, but they do often interact and the good architectural historian, I believe, must be something of a private detective.

A book as diverse as this depends on many kinds of sources and a few people who have been immensely helpful. Above all it has been aided, even partly shaped, by my director Robin Lough who, with Robert McNab, came to me with the idea of a film on Frank Lloyd Wright and others of his stature. I felt that yet another television showing of the 'masterbuilders' would be redundant, unless they were connected to the present. So Robin and I worked out a series, matching eight Pre-Modernists with eight Post-Modernists, with the idea that this would bring the past alive and give the present more weight and dimension. Future pairings—Otto Wagner and Hans Hollein, Antonio Gaudí and Ricardo Bofill for example—will, I hope, give this comparison of periods deeper substance. We are now going through the kind of complex epoch which those just prior to 1920s Modernism faced, of merging the new technologies and social tasks with the older discoveries of architecture.

In researching the life of Frank Lloyd Wright I have made use of the standard works—those of Henry-Russell Hitchcock, Vincent Scully, Norris Kelly Smith and H. Allen Brooks—but above all two stand out: Wright's own *An Autobiography* published in 1932 and 1943 (Quartet Books, London, 1977) and Robert C. Twombly's *Frank Lloyd Wright His Life and His Architecture* (John Wiley and Sons, New York, 1979). Both of these books are excellent sources, especially for Wright's very complicated and fascinating life. I am indebted in equal measure to them and the Taliesin Fellowship for the help and insight they provided into one of the most extraordinarily far-reaching lives that any architect has had the pleasure, and pain, to live. Bruce Pfeiffer was welcoming to me and the BBC and most forthcoming with anecdotes and critical views. We filmed two days at Taliesin East causing some disruption: one of the architects was kind enough to fell several trees—that needed chopping—so we could film the old windmill. Olgivanna Wright was especially kind to give us some time and consent to an interview. Philip Johnson, as will be found in the recorded conversations, provided his usual witty insight into the contemporary scene. He allowed us to take over his Glass House one afternoon to film several conversations with Michael Graves and himself. For this I am most grateful as I am for the kindness he has continued to show me, in spite of our widely divergent views.

Several people provided information over the years, but the exact provenance is now lost to my memory. Michael Graves, a long-time friend, no doubt influenced my views and not only about himself, but it would be difficult to specify exactly how, since our talks have gone on for so long. In any case this book and the film have benefited from his forthcoming candour, especially when talking about his own life. Thomas Beeby, the Chicago architect, provided me with fascinating material and my wife, Maggie Keswick, provided me the usual critical help editing things down to manageable and, perhaps, more elegant proportions. Thomas A. Hines very helpfully suggested that we film the William E. Martin Residence and arranged for us to do so. A film, like a building, is necessarily a collaborative affair and unless everyone is working in a certain harmony, the work of all will suffer. Thus I'm particularly happy to acknowledge the professional skill and amusing company of the BBC film unit: John McGlashan, Rosemarie Bradford, Niall Kennedy and John Murphy. They, along with Arthur Bennett in the cutting room, were always vigilant and cheerful over a long and arduous period. Finally a word of thanks to my publisher Andreas Papadakis, and to my editors Frank Russell and Kelly Crossman, for producing this book at such short notice.

Charles Jencks, London

PRE-MODERNISM AND POST-MODERNISM

No person who is not a great sculptor or painter can *be an architect. If he is not a sculptor or painter, he can only be a builder.*
John Ruskin, *Lectures on Architecture and Painting.*

IN 1933, THE SWISS ARCHITECT LE CORBUSIER, IN A SOMEWHAT desperate mood, justified Modern architecture because it was safer from aerial bombardment than traditional cities. The high slab blocks, he argued, would present less of a target for explosives than a spread out city.[1] Modern Architecture could be scientifically proved to be the safest style, and it would also save the world through mass-housing. But it wasn't an enemy from outside which gave a new twist to the argument and showed Modern housing to be lacking in certain kinds of high-energy safety. The dynamite came from within the community. In any number of well-publicised demolitions, filmed from all sorts of angles like Antonioni's *Blow Up*, the local inhabitants, and then the world, watched with a certain aesthetic satisfaction as, in rumbling slow-motion the theory of mass, Modern-estate-living came gently to the ground. Modern Architecture, as a style and ideology, lived happily from 1920 to 1960, a long and fruitful life for any architectural movement. By the mid-70s, with explosions averaging one estate per month in some countries, it had gone into full retreat with its only remaining defenders being a few tenured professors, and misguided idealists, confused by the word 'Modern'.

'Modern' has meant many things to many people since it first gained popularity among architects as long ago, surprisingly, as the Renaissance.[2] Above all it has meant being up-to-date, current or contemporary. In short, 'relevant'. In the 1920s, however, the word took on more specific meanings, becoming associated with a manner—'The International Style'—and an ideology of avant-gardism, a touching belief that social progress could be promoted by technical invention and pure reason. At this point, the full Western tradition of architecture was jettisoned for being reactionary: not only ornament and symbolism were thrown out, but traditional patterns of city living, the 'rooms' of the town known as squares, and enclosed streets.

Oh, Brave New World of glass and steel, freed of superstition and Popery, snobbism and Corinthian Capitals, led by fearless technocrats and selfless engineers so noble in their democratic altruism!

The *Nouveau Monde* has indeed got its Modern Movement and its teams of objective technocrats, but somehow things are not much better than they were in the old Capitalist cities. Instead of being ruled by aristocrats, they are administered by bureaucrats, and the International Style has become the perfect, natural expression of this bureaucracy. It is *this* Modern Architecture which is on the retreat, the austere manner of the nine-to-five functionaries, who have no time for art, ornament, humour or sensuous pleasure in buildings: no enjoyment of all the visual and tactile elements which the Western tradition of architecture used to sanction.

Paradoxically, it is two architects, who sometimes called themselves Modern, that have fought against this: the *Pre*-Modernist Frank Lloyd Wright and the *Post*-Modernist Michael Graves. Like others who have come before and after the Modern Movement—for instance, Otto Wagner and Hans Hollein in Austria—they have had the courage to uphold an artistic approach which includes the full repertoire of traditional elements, and still combine this with current technology and social realism. In short, they have steered a very careful course between the two sterilities which have played such havoc in this century: straight revivalism and avant-gardism.

Wright and Graves could stand against these, and other, doctrines because they could *draw* their vision of architecture with conviction, and convince society that their view was desirable. Architectural power grows out of the barrel of a 4B pencil, and those who can wield it reign, like monarchs, over their profession. Frank Lloyd Wright spent sixty years as the self-proclaimed king of American architecture, an artist-architect in the grand manner, whose credibility as a ruler was sustained as much by his visual competence as it was by his 'honest arrogance'. His reign has passed to Michael Graves, who is holding off pretenders to the throne who can't draw or paint as well as he. In any century except our own these visual skills would be assumed; but because good architects must be good businessmen, or practical, or adept at organisation, their drawing skills are regarded with suspicion, if not actually attacked. And this has led to the unfortunate paradox which Wright and Graves have exploited: for the fortunate few, who can think creatively with their pencil and also build, architectural power is immense. Fewer and fewer artist-architects reign over more and more followers, or at least influence ever greater numbers. The sad jokes about 'Wright-clones' and 'Graves-clones' are not, alas, without foundation.

Pre-Modernism, the synthesis of Modern technology and building tasks with traditional architecture into a hybrid language. J. M. Olbrich, *Secession Building*, Vienna, 1898-9. Not only did this influence Wright's Unity Temple, but it crystallised that hybrid language partly based on flat, volumetric surfaces and intense decorative incident. The fresh use of classical elements rendered with a new technology is also apparent; even the symbolic programme—the vegetable dome, stylised plants, and owls—is a new version of old themes.

Otto Wagner, *Post Office Savings Bank*, Vienna, 1904-6. Wagner's previous classical revivalism has been transformed, but is still recognisable behind the new technology. The piers have a traditional base, shaft and capital (of lights), while the mechanical ducts also have a tripartite division. This 'High-Tech Order' remains a paradigm for Post-Modernists since it actually orders the whole building in plan and elevation; the exterior is a transformation of Greek and Roman themes in aluminium. Clearly Wagner is *the* Free Style Classicist, combining Western tradition and the imperatives of the new.

Josef Hoffmann, *Palais Stoclet*, Brussels 1905-11. Like other Pre-Modernist work this hybrid architecture influenced that of Wright and Graves. Flat unadorned surfaces are in maximum contrast with decorative mouldings of a new type; the symbolic accentuation of entrance and tower with human and vegetal figures looks to the Greek past and heroic, secular future: are these the new race of Nietzschean supermen?

And here lies yet another paradox: the influence of the artist-architect has grown in proportion to the decline of art in architecture. It's impossible to measure this with any accuracy, but a rough feeling for this trend can be obtained by comparing the amount of money a society is willing to spend in adorning its significant buildings with ornament, sculpture, crafted details and painting—the spice of architecture. At the Parthenon they spent 80% of the budget on the gold and ivory statue of Athena, the frieze, sculpture groups and stelae (which is why they have largely disappeared). At Chartres 65% of the budget went into the stained glass and excellent column sculpture (the architects sacrificed several towers for these); today artists are fighting, in state commissions, to get a mere 1%. Garbage disposal gets more than that. Any culture which drops below 5% for its honorific building tasks should be called just a civilisation, and probably that's too good a name for it. Wright was fond of saying that America had passed from barbarism to degeneracy without having

Frank Lloyd Wright, *Studio*, Oak Park, 1895-7. Symmetrical figures form an implicit capital which culminates in a vegetal abacus. Wright like the Secessionists was interested in revitalising symbolic ornamant.

gone through culture, but if the crude index of money is anything to go by, then all post-industrial countries are Late-Decadent, perhaps 'Too Late, Late-Decadent'.

Frank Lloyd Wright and Michael Graves have fought all the way to keep architecture an art and a role for the artist in buildings, and for this they have paid a price: continual conflicts, punishing hard work, divorce. Even lack of recognition at times. But the drive for a total art remained their goal, and perhaps solace, in spite of constant domestic stress. To unearth the story behind the leaders of the most public of arts is to necessarily touch, from time to time, on private matters, and this book will examine areas that are usually disregarded when architecture is discussed. I don't believe we should ignore the human story when two such emotionally and intellectually committed artists are involved.

It's interesting that we are entering a period when architects and the public are looking back to their roots. This means, for Westerners whose culture was disrupted by the 'great experiment' of Modernism, the period just prior to 1914. Then the protagonists wanted to be 'Modern'—Otto Wagner, the Germans and the French avant-garde had used the word positively for 20 years—but they also kept an equal regard for tradition. They were at the crucial turning point, when mass-society, new technologies, styles, and sensibilities were being formulated. But they realised their value had to be challenged by the old. Thus the peculiar tension in their work we find so vital today, the complexity, richness, and commitment to detail. They wanted a meaningful dialogue between the present and past. We want it today. The Pre-Modernists achieved it with a *hybrid* language often called 'Free Style', 'Art Nouveau' or 'Secession'; the Post-Modernists are achieving it with a Free Style Classicism. In both cases the demands of present reality—all the technical, social and cultural aspects which were called 'Modern'—were tied with the greater Western tradition. For the dual concerns and hybrid styles we need *double-barreled* labels like Pre- and Post-Modernism. They may be unwieldy, or ugly, but they refer to the continuity of Western culture in a period of disjunction.

❋❋❋

THE *SPIRIT* OF TRADITION— FRANK LLOYD WRIGHT (1867-1959)

WHEN FRANK LLOYD WRIGHT WAS BORN IN RURAL WISCONSIN IN 1867 the United States was not yet one hundred years old. The American Civil War had recently ended, and the population was mostly engaged in farming. Wright has described, in *An Autobiography*, how he spent the summers working on his uncle's farm, learning the lesson of self-reliance through 'manly work'. He managed to turn a monotonous task of hauling and pitching hay into something imaginative by transforming repetitious motion into music: 'I would actually sing to the ever-recurring monotonies of rhythm . . . . Here was the secret of endurance for the imaginative.'[3] Later on he was to turn the repetitions of architectural form into 'an edifice of sound'. The notion of architecture as frozen music he may have picked up, not from Goethe, but his father. William C. Wright was always entertaining at the piano.

Frank Lloyd Wright has credited his father for giving him a taste for Bach and Beethoven, but obviously a liking for popular Victorian songs as well: 'Tis Sweet to Meet, and Each Other Greet' was one melody his father composed and sold as sheet music. William Wright must have also given his son a taste for continuous moving: he was an itinerant preacher, and when this didn't prove financially rewarding he became a school teacher, lawyer and 'politician, moving more than thirty times in his life. 'Wright the Nomad' might have been the family motto, or 'Wright the Polymath', or 'Wright the Populist': the crowds who came to hear the great orator at the Richland Center Baptist Society were like the crowds Frank Lloyd Wright was later to draw on: Fundamentalist, deeply feeling, direct and simple. All the chapter headings in *An Autobiography* read like his father's Baptist sermons: instead of his father's 'The Art of Happiness' there is 'A Song to Heaven', 'An Angry Prophecy and a Preachment: The City'; 'The First Protestant Affirmation', 'Truth is Life'. While he later became a

Rolling Wisconsin countryside, valley of 'The God Almighty Joneses', Spring Green. View from Taliesin towards the pond and Windmill.

Joseph Lyman Sillsbee, *Unity Chapel*, Hillside, Wisconsin, 1886. Wright later worked for Sillsbee, and he apparently supervised part of the construction of this open plan, 'organic' building.

Hillside Home School, Hillside, Wisconsin, 1887. Eclectic, Queen Anne Revival, or Shingle Style buildings constitute the first period of experiment in Wright's work. The concern for hybrid elements and flowing space remained constant, although the specific style continued to change. (Photo: State Historical Society of Wisconsin)

city sophisticate, he never entirely lost his fundamentalist religion.

Because William Wright left his wife Anna Lloyd-Jones and filed for a divorce in 1885, the young son developed a stronger and more lasting relationship with her. In fact he credited her with steering him into architecture, and no doubt she also gave him the sense of fierce independence which characterised the Lloyd-Joneses. Like the proverbial Jewish mother she provided the bulwark on which he rested for strength, especially when later he too was ostracised for divorce. Significantly, she gave him Froebel blocks to play with which taught him the lessons of integrating structure, construction and space into a unity he would later call 'organic' (because indivisible like living tissue). In fashioning this concept of organic unity, he was actually being extremely conservative, insisting on a principle of integration which had been commonplace since Aristotle's *Poetics* and the writings on architecture of Vitruvius and Alberti. Wright always reaffirmed the *spirit* of tradition, often against the *letter*, and this sometimes made him think he was being revolutionary, or modern, or more of a loner than he really was.

At nineteen, the year after his father left home for good, the young Frank supervised the building of the Joneses' Unity Chapel, a structure which still stands today in the heart of the clan's territory, and next to which Frank, Mrs Cheney and other members of the family are buried. The building was designed by Joseph Lyman Sillsbee, an adept Chicago follower of the Queen Anne Eclectic Style, and it has many of the hallmarks of 'organic' architecture: a simplicity or unity of materials appropriate to a Unitarian chapel, an horizontal emphasis created by a high water table or plinth, and lintels flush with the soffit, a Japanese emphasis on the size of the roof, and an open, flowing plan.[4]

The next year, in 1887, Wright carried out his own first commission, also in a wooden version of the eclectic, Queen Anne Style: the Hillside Home school. Set in the farmlands of his Welsh clan, this had the wide, simple gables and horizontal emphasis of his later work, but it was also very much in keeping with the nearby Sillsbee Chapel. It was built for his two maiden aunts, Nell and Jane Lloyd-Jones: the clan always supported its members, as it did in the old country. And significantly, the school had for its crest the family's motto 'Truth Against the World'. This motto Wright was to adopt sometimes as the ostracised architect or romantic lover, or other times as the Welsh bard incarnate—*Taliesin*—the mythical poet who would stand up as the country seer against the conventional, court poets.[5]

His aunts also asked him to build a windmill overlooking the reservoir and the rolling landscape that surrounded them. But a local builder condemned Wright's wooden design saying a sixty foot tower would 'Blow down sure as death and taxes'. Almost a century later it still stands, a bit weatherbeaten and resurfaced, but none the less proud and defiant, proof of the structural stability of the interlocked forms: he called the tall diamond 'Romeo' and the surrounding octagon, 'Juliet'. Each form, Wright said, was 'indispensable to the other'. 'Romeo', he proclaimed in a nicely turned architectural metaphor, would 'do all the work', while 'Juliet' would cuddle alongside to support and exalt him. Romeo takes the side of the blast and Juliet will entertain the school children. Let's 'let it go at that, no symbol should be taken too far . . . .'[6] Designing a building around a symbol, and naming it, was a traditional piece of architectural art that Wright never let die—and one that is being revived today by Post-Modernists.

In order to study architecture and learn the traditional, classical language, Wright, the country boy, had to go first to the nearby city, Madison, and then the metropolis, Chicago—the fastest growing, biggest and toughest meat-market in the world. Nothing could be further from the natural rhythm of the Wisconsin farmlands than the mechanised slaughter of ten million cattle per year, the horror, stench and brutality of which were described by many writers of the time. But Chicago still *was* the place for a romantic with an over-riding ambition, and the opposition of rural simplicity and city sophistication was to prove a positive antithesis as it was later for Michael Graves. In Chicago, Wright worked for several architectural offices until he finally found a job with the most cultured architect of the Mid-West, Louis Sullivan. While working on key buildings for Sullivan and Adler, he also started an illicit practice of architecture at night, 'bootlegging' houses away from the office and sharpening his own

Romeo and Juliet Windmill, Spring Green, Wisconsin, 1896. Horizontal boards and battens have replaced the original shingle forms, but the Froebel integration of structure, construction and volume is still apparent.

Charnley House, Chicago, 1892. Free Style Classicism is apparent in this hybrid building which mixes several traditions. Admired by Modernists for its flat planes and horizontal massing, it's of equal interest for its geometric ornament and contrasting scales and materials.
(Photo: Chicago Historical Society)

Nathan Moore Residence, Oak Park, Illinois, 1895, rebuilt after a fire, 1923. Gigantic roof forms intersect with a large chimney, and encompass various styles appropriate to their task.

eclectic mixture of Sillsbee, Queen Anne and Sullivan classicism. His Charnley House of 1892 is a perfect amalgamation of these sources into his own version of Free Style Classicism.

Just before his twenty-second birthday, in 1889, he married Catherine Lee Tobin, the daughter of a wealthy businessman, and together with Sullivan and his other contacts she gave him the cultural background he lacked; she gave him social polish as well.[7] They joined the River Forest Tennis Club, competed annually in the horse show, and settled in the exclusive, Protestant neighbourhood of Oak Park, west of the seedy part of Chicago, 'where the saloon stops and the church steeple begins'. Here, in an idyllic American suburb, with giant oaks, sprawling lawns and no fences (as one would find in Europe), Wright built some sixty rambling homes by the year 1900 (when he forged the 'Prairie Style'). In their sensitive eclecticism they fitted perfectly the comfortable assumptions of middle class life.

The Nathan Moore house, 1895, (rebuilt 1923 after a fire) is one of the best of this period—although Wright was later to think it one of his worst. It uses different styles—he was later to regard as a 'sham'—in various and appropriate ways to give character to different parts of the building. The cosy inglenook is sheltered suitably behind the Gothic windows; the magnificent formal garden, for entertainment, is framed by grand classical elements; a sense of domesticity is created by the half-timbered Tudor, often the sign of homestead; and then the Indian finials, or totem poles, or whatever one wishes to call the Secessionist masts, indicate the former presence of the great plains Indians, and the melting pot that is Chicago. As with Otto Wagner, the other great Pre-Modernist, the notion of eclecticism was repugnant because it was associated with dull revivalism, indeed it was used interchangeably as a word for copying. In spite of this linguistic anomaly, in spite of

Wright's condemnation of 'fashion and sham', I would argue that his buildings often succeed to the extent that they are eclectic. The same idea has been put by the historian Rudolf Wittkower when he says all great architects tend to be great eclectics because they transform pre-existing themes.[8]

Frank Lloyd Wright's own house and studio, built 1889-1895 and later, became the laboratory for many of his experiments in domestic architecture. On the exterior he again mixed several styles and geometries—some of the detail might even incorporate Welsh decoration—while the interior uses a free-flowing space to tie together public places: the entrance hall, stairway and living room. Queen Anne Revival designers had evolved a similar spatial flow and unity, around the same elements, but what gave Wright's combination its special quality was its formation around the *symbol* of family unity: the fireplace, the hearth, the place where the group would meet at least once a day to celebrate the sacrament of fraternity. This was the ideal Wright had learned from the Lloyd-Joneses.

For twenty years he brought up a thriving family of six children upstairs, and ran a thriving architectural practice of twelve or so draughtsmen downstairs. He was very much the father of both families, giving each one their central hearth. For the rest of his life the

Dining Room. An Arts and Crafts emphasis on well-detailed wood, joinery and ornament is tied to an hieratic emphasis on the table: it's almost a piece of architecture, or a high altar.

Frank Lloyd Wright Residence, Oak Park, 1889-1893, flowing space around central hearth. Characteristically an inglenook is to either side, a motto, 'Truth is life', is over the fireplace and a place for dried flowers is reserved, rather like the tokonoma in a Japanese house. (Photo: Curt Teich & Co., Chicago)

Studio Hearth with its uplifting proverb above the fire—an archetype of family, or communal existence, since the camp fire was enshrined by Beaux-Arts doctrine. (Photo: Curt Teich & Co, Chicago)

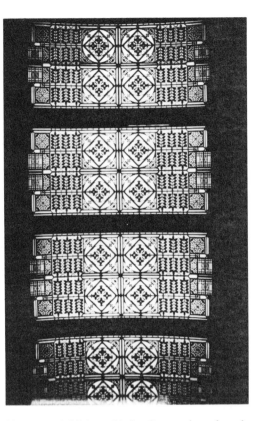

fireplace represented the unity of the family, the clan, and often carried an uplifting moral similar to that of the Lloyd-Joneses ('Truth is Life' above his own hearth). The artistic celebration of domestic life gave Wright's architecture a special flavour. The collective dining table was almost as important as the fireplace, and it was treated as a high altar, accompanied by throne-like chairs and, overhead, a symbol of growing life. Art was in every detail of the other collective space, the children's playroom. The lights with their Japanese-like brackets and paper; the stained glass around the inglenook, which is too small for an adult to stand in (Wright loved placing a low space next to the high). Then that large, over-arching space itself, a cross between a Roman barrel-vault and a Japanese black-and-white temple, has its mural of Aladdin's lamp at the end. The story was a favourite of Wright, when he was a child, and here he has worked with the artist, Orlando Gianninni, to abstract out a decorative motif: the genie that hovers above is one of the first *abstract* representations of Wright's career. He realised that architecture isn't complete until it has a painting or sculpture to point up its meaning and that the most successful environmental art is an object that is both abstract, like architectural rhythm, and figurative, like traditional painting. The feeling that pervades these spaces, even today, is that of a large,

Playroom Addition with its Roman barrel-vault and abstract representation of the children's story *Aladdin's Lamp*. A piano and minstrels' gallery, in miniature, are at the other end—both of them turned into architectural jokes quite suitable for children. A cut-out, fretwork pattern of Gothic and natural forms allows a subdued light to filter from above.

enjoyable family surrounding themselves with art, the growing plants that would be placed carefully in copper vases, and the noise of life. A son remembers 'clambakes, tea parties in his studio, cotillions in the large drafting room . . . . There were parties somewhere all of the time and everywhere some of the time.'[9] The architecture both symbolises and entails a family stability, as if Wright were trying to prove himself a father who wouldn't leave his children. After 1900 and his local success, Wright became immensely more ambitious and decided to take on the European avant-garde, whose work he must have known well through magazines. He fashioned a new form of horizontal *streamlining*—a word he claims to have invented, and then helped form a group of architects, the 'Chicago Eighteen', which soon evolved into the 'New School of the Middle West'.

The Prairie House was the result of both efforts. Long stretching lines of wood trim, often black set against a white plaster background, as at the William E. Martin residence, were meant to suggest the open horizon of the Chicago prairie, and the continuous streamline of the machine. Again abstraction was to be representational, the symbol not 'taken too far', but still present as a suggestion. Wright wrote that the 'Prairie house exterior recognises the influence of the prairie, is firmly and broadly associated with the site and makes a feature of its quiet level, through low terraces and broad eaves'.[10] This revolutionary message, partly the new machine aesthetic, was offered up not as a Futurist *Messagio*, a broadsheet printed on proletariat newspaper, but in the pages of *The Ladies Home Journal*! A few months before, Wright had attacked the degenerate taste of the American architect who 'panders to silly women his silly artistic sweets', who cuts his cloth in Louis XIV style, to suit his commercialised clients. Now, in effect, Wright was appealing to just such clients, in their own organ of conventionality. The matrons of Middle America were going to lead the aesthetic shock-troops over the next visual barrier. As *The Ladies Home Journal* put it: 'A Home in a Prairie Town'—'the Fifth Design in the Journal's New Series of Model Suburban Houses which can be built at Moderate Cost', $7,000—was meant to appeal directly to the good economic sense and propriety of the upper-middle class. William E. Martin, part owner of the 'E-Z Polish Factory' (also designed by Wright) was just such an enlightened client, a captain of industry.

Today the house still has those qualities Wright specifies for the Prairie Home: 'The ground plan is arranged to offer least resistance to a simple mode of living in keeping with a *high ideal of the family life together* . . . cement and metal lath is suggested for the exterior covering throughout because it is simple and . . . *durable and cheap* . . . . The interior is plastered throughout . . . and trimmed all

William E. Martin Residence, Oak Park, 1902. The porch stretches into the garden, while black lines of trim and ribbon windows cut up the volumes into horizontal streamlines.

Martin Residence, interior focus down passageway with Secessionist 'art glass' overhead, hearth to the left, dining to the right, and painting, decoration and sculpture accentuating the route.

Ward Willits House, Highland Park, Illinois, 1901-2. The mature Prairie House shows a Japanese emphasis on wood left in its natural, dark hue contrasting with white surfaces and decorative glass. The classical symmetries are tied to a central hearth in a pinwheel manner.

through with flat boards of Georgia pine . . . all the wood should be *shellacked* once and waxed and the plaster should be stained with *thin, pure colour*,[11] (my italics). And, of course, all the black horizontals represent the simplicity of machine production, the streamline, as well as the flat prairie. In addition to all these qualities the flowing space and extensive use of 'art glass', or geometrical coloured glass, was characteristic. By 1902, almost all of his buildings had the exaggerated procession from the street, back and forth through tight spaces, to culminate in the hearth and dining table.

Wright applied the same general principles of space and streamlining to public buildings. Even the New Prairie Style was conceived for a domestic scale. This style in fact owed something to Europe and Japan, the machine aesthetic of Otto Wagner, the writings of Oscar Wilde, the Arts and Crafts Movement of England and the black and white drawing style of Beardsley and Hiroshige. But all these sources were turned into an original, eclectic whole, and offered up as the new '*American*' democratic style, the style which would keep the country free from the domination of Europe. The Larkin Administration Building, built for a soap and mail order company, was the pretext for this national statement: 'the American flag is the only flag that would look well on or in this building . . . I think our building is wholly American in its directness and freshness of treatment. It wears no badge of servitude to foreign "styles" . . . .'[12]

Russell Sturgis, the foremost American critic, reviewed the Larkin Building in the major American magazine, the *Architectural Record*, and found it 'extremely ugly . . . a monster of awkwardness' because it didn't have a delicate and moving 'light, shade and colour'.[13] He, like Wright, was looking for a 'living style of architecture' and, in spite of his censorious remarks, found that the Larkin Building 'puts on a new aspect'. However, it lacked historic detail, particularly that of the Italian Renaissance, which Sturgis favoured. Wright, in his reply, printed in a company pamphlet of 1909, defines his principles as carrying forward the *spirit*, rather than the letter of tradition:

> There is a common chord in all this that will be heard; and it is not a plea for ugliness. It is a plea for first principles—for less heat and parasitism, and more light and pragmatic integrity; for less architecture in quotation marks and more engineering.[14]

'Pragmatic integrity' refers not only to the *functional* expression of air shafts and stairs, but also to the new social order and its new industrial building tasks, the commercial factories, the 'bread-winning operations' that John Ruskin had condemned as 'hostile to art'. This hostility to commercial realism had left a 'train of reactionaries' setting back the course of architecture 'twenty-five years'; Wright's mentor

The Larkin Administration Building, Buffalo, New York, 1903-6 (destroyed), view from the factory side. Note the spartan decorative elements including globes and putti. (Photo: The Museum of Modern Art, New York)

Sullivan had put the mark at 'fifty years', becase of the revivalist exhibition in Chicago, 1893.

In his counter-attack on Sturgis, Wright also defends a type of ornament which articulates 'the elements of structure, and is tolerable in composition only when saying something pertinent'. Significant as opposed to gratuitous ornament, he points out at Sturgis's expense, is evident on the interior piers, where the galleries drop back to reveal 'capitals', allow more light and space, and give 'rhythm to the arrangement when otherwise it would have lacked it'. This functional and aesthetic one-upmanship must have pleased Wright, for he knew he was beating Sturgis at his own game of classicism—of keeping the spirit of classicism alive by transforming it with the new requirements. He thrusts home the point, the interpretation which at once puts his Free Style Classicism at the centre of the Western tradition, and Sturgis' revivalism to the side as a dead style.

> Meanwhile, the superficial observer obsessed by the *letter* of tradition says it is ugly. The man in whom the *spirit* of tradition still lives, the man who looks deeper and into the future, has said it is inspiring. Well! It was built for the man who for the sake of the future, gets underneath, and not for the man who, startled, clutches his lifeless traditions closer to his would-be-conservative breast and shrieks, 'It is ugly!'[15]

Looked at in the *spirit* of tradition, we can see it as having a cathedral shape with the central windows expressing the large, interior nave space and the side towers expressing the galleries, or aisles. This, his first 'cathedral to work' even had the uplifting moral placed on axis, on-high: 'Seek and ye shall find . . . '. In effect then it is not just a cathedral, but one of his Prairie Homes, built vertically not horizontally, and with the ornament and proverb decorating the source of light, enlightenment, rather than the hearth. Wright was later to interpret it as the first example of the Machine Aesthetic, ahead of the Futurists and Le Corbusier, an *American* invention, which 'was in every detail practical or it was only another sentimentality to further demoralise the country'.[16] When Wright condemned sentimentality, as he did several times in his life, he usually did so in a context referring to the thoughtless application of period styles, the finery appropriate to one age being misapplied to another, because of the confused sentiments of a rootless nation. In this he was reflecting a European view of America, and it's ironic that today, it is precisely a sentimentality that Michael Graves has found in his early drawings and renderings. In one of our first conversations on Wright we disputed this very point.

Michael Graves: I don't often look at Wright's drawings. The colour

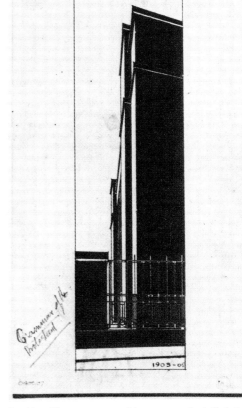

drawings especially, because I find them so overly sweet.

CJ: Really? Sentimental?

MG: Yes, and I suppose that's probably the spirit of the age, that there is that kind of golden glow to everything . . . the distinction I would see in the drawing styles of Wright and Le Corbusier is that the latter would insist that you see the buildings as a set of *ideas* first.

CJ: Rather than an image of the finished building?

MG: Rather than trying to imitate the buildings. Wright's plans are, however, quite incredible in the conceptual sense.

CJ: Well, he *did* make some conceptual drawings too.

MG: Of course he did.

CJ: I mean his unsentimental building, which he called 'the first emphatic Protestant in architecture'. He actually labelled a drawing 'the grammar of the Protestant' and that's a conceptual sketch if ever there was one. It's about volume, light and shadow.

MG: But I find the sweetness of some of Wright's pictures to be off-putting.

CJ: But surely the perspectives give a very clear idea of what the

Larkin Nave, space with geometrical lighting fixtures given an ornamental treatment top and bottom, along with a Secessionist ornament invented by Wright. The Classical organisation has been obscured by the emphasis on the new elements such as the fireproofing, air-conditioning and metal furniture, but note the traditional bay rhythms and the homily on top. (Photo: The Museum of Modern Art, New York)

'The Grammar of the Protestant', a conceptual sketch reworked from a photograph taken close up with perspective correction.

building is going to look like *in the best light*. And that's why photographers invariably find themselves photographing the building from the point that he drew them.

Such drawings, as that of the next 'Protestant' scheme—conveniently for a Unitarian church—impose a diagonal perspective view, the best one to display volumes rushing away from each other in maximum counterpoint. This was the view favoured by Beaux-Arts renderers— indeed the Parthenon is first viewed from such an angle, below, so that its lines rush off in opposite directions, and *most* of the building can thereby be understood. So Wright is again using the spirit of tradition to dramatise his first, most accomplished, essay in cubic composition. Again it was a *protest* against the sentimentality of previous styles. No church spires pointing to heaven here, Wright insisted, but a wonderful concrete, boxy temple, like the Froebel blocks Wright had played with as a child—simple, logical and austere. Like the Larkin building, the Froebel blocks have generated a cruciform of space in plan, section and elevation: an 'organic *unity*' of design, necessitated in part by the extremely low cost. For $45,000 all Wright could do was design a shuttering form for the concrete and rotate it, imaginatively, around the site.[17]

On the inside the Unity Temple has, I believe, the most profound interior space built in America up to that time. Original, strong and entirely suited to its Unitarian message of unity and abstract harmony, it bears comparison with the Pantheon in Rome for inspiring a sense of cosmic awe in the believer and atheist alike. The mysterious light filtering through the coffered grid overhead is perfectly balanced by the ingenious spatial interlocking: some seven levels of space and light flow into the central hall.

The brilliance of Wright was to produce a new architecture that was at the same time very old. His cool cream piers, with their dark mouldings, remind one of Michelangelo's Laurentian Chapel—equally charged with dynamic lines—but Wright puts the mouldings not on the edges to stop the eye, as a classicist would, but across volumes to break up and reunite them in a new way. The overlapping volume, the lap joint, the moving lines all became ideas of later Modernist design—De Stijl and the Constructivists. No wonder Wright claimed to have invented Modern Architecture twenty years before its official birth with the International Style.

And yet was Wright really a Modern architect in the accepted sense of that word? He started an article in 1908 with the pronouncement: 'Radical though it may be [my work] is dedicated to the cause conservative . . . to that elemental law and order inherent in all great architecture'.[18] 'Law and Order?' 'Cause conservative?' By now

Unity Church, Oak Park, 1904, drawing and present state. The Unity Temple to the left, inscribed in a Greek cross, and the Unity House, the parish house to the right. Free Style Classicism with all the traditional ornaments, lettering and planting slightly altered, simplified and built in monolithic, exposed pebble concrete.

Unity Church, interior corner piers, 'hollow and free-standing ducts' have decorative strips which cross the volumes, not on the edges, but in a manner that flattens the cubes and makes the eye move continuously. The aesthetic was taken up twelve years later by De Stijl artists. Note the light and space, pouring in from various sources, also giving a dynamic movement to a static cube.

Wright had become so successful he was attracting clients like Henry Ford and mass-producing ten palaces a year for those Americans who had worked hard to make it. It's clear that before the First World War he saw himself as a reformist not a Modernist, and that he was renewing the tradition of great architecture 'from within', not starting the Modernist 'Tradition of the New' from without. While his 'Protestant Reformation' may have been, like that of Adolf Loos, against *redundant* ornament, it was certainly not against all ornament, nor indeed all of the elements Modernism was later to expurgate in its 'vacuum-cleaning period'. He had a social view of architecture as we shall see, but it favoured Mini-Capitalism, not State-Socialism. Like other Pre-Modernists—Peter Behrens, Otto Wagner, J. M. Olbrich, Antonio Gaudí, Josef Hoffmann, C. R. Mackintosh, Victor Horta, and H. P. Berlage—he was challenged by contemporary society and technology, but saw them as a spur to tradition, not a substitute for it.

✳✳✳

BY THE AGE OF FORTY-ONE, IN 1908, WRIGHT HAD ACHIEVED BOTH A social and professional success extraordinary for a country farm boy. Yet a confusing doubt was beginning to grow, a malaise which had opposite causes not unconnected with the relation of Modernism to

Western traditional architecture: suburban conformity in Oak Park, the burdens of a domestic scene with his own six boisterous children, and a rather conventional wife who had to devote more time to bringing them up than appreciating his architectural genius. She, previously the cultivated one, had become domesticated. And then there was the lack of any deep architectural criticism: he either received censorship, such as the Sturgis article, or uncritical adulation. His rage at not finding a kindred spirit, or sympathetic understanding, can be judged by a response to Harriet Monroe, a poet and critic who, in a review of the Architecture Club's 1907 Exhibition, found his two most important buildings, Larkin and Unity, to be 'without grace or ease or monumental beauty'. She praised his houses, but this was not enough. Wright had to answer her in a letter:

> Personally, I am hungry for the honest genuine criticism that searches the soul of the thing and sifts its form. Praise isn't needed especially. There is enough of that, such as it is, but we all need intelligent painstaking inquiry leading into the nature of the proposition to be characterised before, with airy grace, the subject is lightly touched up with House Beautiful English for the Mob.[19]

He reiterates, in this letter, the distinction between the letter and spirit of tradition: 'Need I say that it is the very spirit that gave life to the old forms that [my] work courts? That it is the true inspiration that made of the time-honoured precedent, in its own time, a living thing that it craves.' He ends the letter on the same note, hoping that the 'first class passenger' (the American upper class) will finally understand that his forms are not 'eccentric', as the newspapers say, but rather 'truly classic in the best sense of that much abused term'.[20]

If Wright was then not fighting a Modernist battle, but on the contrary fighting to be recognised as a 'true classic', we can see why his doubts would lead him to take drastic action. In the same letter he refers to an idea that was becoming uppermost in his mind, the Cause of American Architecture, something he was to turn into a quasi-religious, *cause celèbre*. The idea is formulated almost as a Baptist sermon by his father:

> Personally, again, I have met little more than the superficial snap-judgment-insult of the 'artistically informed'. I am quite used to it, glad to owe it nothing in any final outcome. But, meanwhile, the Cause suffers delay![21]

The Cause of American Architecture was now his personal responsibility; to regenerate it in Spirit, with the first principles of Classic Architecture, not its Letter—which was to be purged as 'Fakery and Sham'. Wright continued to write 'In the Cause of Architecture' for *The Architectural Record*—1908, a new version 1914, then 1923 and

Mamah Borthwick Cheney, photograph from the period 1911. (Photo: Chicago Tribune)

1927 (in five parts). The message varied, but always contrasted, some version of original, organic architecture—'Truth is Life'—with the 'sentimental' and corrupting 'styles' which ruled the day in America. If the best critics, such as Harriet Monroe, couldn't see this Cause, and if the Europeans could, and did, appreciate Wright's work, then why not leave for Europe—the font of true Architecture?

By 1907, with this Cause failing just as he was formulating it, his despair with America began to grow. He started to shock the Mid-Western moral majority by flaunting married women in his grand, open car. Like a Secessionist 'artiste', he let his hair grow over the collar. He wore expensive clothes, flowing neckties, riding breeches and a Norfolk jacket—not the attire for the Oak Park commuter. He had reached the height of his Prairie School Style; with the Unity Church, he had shown a talent of world class; what could he do next in a provincial suburb?

> About 1909 . . . weary, I was losing my grip on my work and even my interest in it . . . . Because I did not know what I wanted, I wanted to go away. Why not go to Germany and prepare the material for the Wasmuth Monograph . . . . Everything, personal or otherwise, bore heavily down on me, domesticity most of all. What I wanted I did not know. I loved my children. I loved my home. A true home is the finest ideal of man, and yet—well, to gain freedom I asked for a divorce.[22]

Probably the reason he left Catherine and went off to Europe, was not simply to gain 'freedom' from domestic banality, but also freedom from American provinciality. Of equal importance was the new woman in his life, who symbolised positive freedom—Mamah Borthwick Cheney—the wife of a client. She was strong-spirited, beautiful and as independent as he was. Unlike Catherine, she could stand up to his intellectual free-thinking. In fact she was already translating feminist books on free love, from German and Swedish, and promoting the new style of motherhood, on how members of a family shouldn't treat each other as so much personal property.

Their love (and love making) was quite open—amazingly so for a conservative suburb. The neighbour of Edwin Cheney, Margaret Allen, has described the childhood reactions of herself and her sister to this recurrent situation:

> Mr. Wright not only built their home but he fell in love with Mrs. Cheney. When we children became aware of this drama, we would stand up on dollie trunks stored away in Helen's closet with its high windows, and look down into the Cheney living room below to watch the two of them making love. Once mother found us there, giggling and laughing together. 'You must never, never do this

again', she said as she led us out of the closet—closing the door with emphasis. But still we knew that strange things were happening about which father and mother only mentioned in a whisper. One Sunday morning early Mr. Wright came over to borrow cream from Olga, our good-hearted maid. Mother overheard the conversation and went to the kitchen, for she was shocked at his presumption and said: 'I would not tarnish the Sabbath day by giving you cream. You who are breaking the Ten Commandments every day of the week!'[23]

Running off to Europe with Mrs. Cheney, leaving behind a combined total of eight children and two spouses, called on his deepest conviction—a rather exaggerated 'Truth Against the World'? His ultimate romantic view had already taken him so far in architecture: if one followed emotions completely, and if they were 'true', then they could not be misleading. In this case love, physical and intellectual, happily coincided with professional advancement. For if Wright had reached the top of his Mid-Western career, then one way he could augment this was through a European stamp of approval.

Since Wasmuth, the German publisher, wanted to publish high-quality plates of his drawings, he could return triumphant to America with this prestigious European book under one arm, and Mrs. Cheney on the other. America always accepts its outcasts if they are recognised abroad.

No doubt Wright never formulated the politics of the situation so explicit. And things certainly didn't work out this pragmatically when the two adulterers returned to suburbia. The press, the relatives, the neighbours were not only furious but vindictive. Wright and Mrs. Cheney did what any convinced intellectual romantics would do: they tried to justify free love, exactly as the unconventional architecture had been justified—publicly. Wright, with perfect timing and perfect naivety, called a press conference on Christmas Day, 1911, to explain his higher love, his elevated morality that absolved him from the lower considerations of family responsibility, and he connected this with his higher *Cause* of an American architecture. Free love equals organic architecture.

The kind of first principles he enunciated could have come from the feminist literature: 'Only to the degree that marriage is mutual is it decent.' 'Love is not property. To take it so is barbarous'.[24]

The press loved it—although they didn't exactly agree: so Wright called another press conference to convince them; then another, and another . . . every day from Boxing Day to New Year's Eve came another statement clarifying the cause of high-minded adultery. The editor of *The Weekly Home News* put the opposite, majority, opinion:

No man and no woman can live in the relation which these two brazenly flaunt and explain it to law-abiding, God-fearing people without 'insulting decency' . . . . [Wright's justifications were] more advertising than his knee-panties, long hair and other funny ways . . . .[25]

The phrase about advertising hurt because it was too near the truth—and one that he would actually exploit forty years later as he became the great American sensationalist architect. But there is no doubt that Wright was sincere in his beliefs, and their universality—the way they might liberate other clandestine lovers behind their Edwardian lace curtains. His articles that used to be titled 'In the Cause of Architecture' now become, implicitly, 'In the Cause of Justifying my Free Religious and Marital Beliefs'. His Free Style Classicism coincided with Free Style ethics.

This crisis produced a change in style, a change in philosophy. Wright, previously the Grand Duke of Suburbia, became Wright the Persecuted World Citizen, moving continuously, sometimes hiding from the law, and building only thirty-four commissions in the next twenty-one years. The first thing he did was to retreat to his family homestead and build a fortress for Mrs. Cheney and himself, a defensive bastion in the wilderness from which they could fight off the onslaught of big-city morality—the press, the moral majority's right to pry. As Wright said later, in an NBC film, his protective mother had prepared a site in the low hills, which had protruding rock ledges:

My people were Welsh . . . . All had Welsh names for their places—my sister's house was called 'Tanyderi', 'under the oaks', so I, too, chose a Welsh name for mine, and it was 'Taliesin'. Taliesin, a Druid, was a member of King Arthur's Round Table. He sang the glories of fine art—I guess he was about the only Britisher who ever did—so I chose Taliesin for a name. It means 'shining brow', and this place, now called Taliesin, is built like a brow on the edge of a hill—not on top of the hill—because I believe you should never build on top of anything directly.[26]

This 'marrying' of the building and hill became the first principle of organic architecture—a building which is '*of* not *on* the hill'—a principle he was later to contradict. In any case, the complex way it nestles in nature, and forms labyrinthine spaces, can be compared not only to a Welsh fortress, but even more to an elaborate, and complex, Chinese garden. Interlocking space cells form a seamless web of open and closed vistas that integrate site, architecture, walls, pools and sculpture. The complexity and ambiguity one associates with Chinese gardens is created by making every space overlap with another, yet be divided by screens, levels, or planting.

Newspaper Headlines, August 20, 1914.

Mamah Borthwick Cheney, grave next to Frank Lloyd Wright and others of the family, 1914.

Unfortunately Wright also had another principle of architecture—one door for all purposes—that was to abet the most tragic act that can befall anyone. The tragedy occurred when he was away from Taliesin East designing Midway Gardens, an entertainment park back in Chicago. He received a telephone call which stunned him with even greater force than the moral majority could possibly have wished: parts of Taliesin had burned to the ground. He hurried back by train, but the newspapers got their first, and printed the even uglier truth.

A Barbados servant who, they said, was underpaid and driven mad by the unconventional lovers, had executed a revenge. He started a fire during lunch and stood by the only escape door, and then murdered, one by one, seven people, among them Mrs. Cheney and two of her children. The horror of this act was too great for even an outraged public to find welcome, although it did seem to some—as the newspapers show—a just retribution for sin.

Wright himself was so overwhelmed that it took him ten years to recover his confidence and return to a more stable existence. He paid tribute to Mrs. Cheney, his greatest love, the one for whom he had thrown away a normal career, by building her the simplest grave. He had a plain casket made from white pine. Then for symbolic decoration he cut every flower in her garden to fill the simple box. This, the most spartan and organic of all his architectural acts, was free from any of the conventional ornament associated with death. Today the grave, with just her name, dates, and the planted tree, conveys the frightening simplicity of a Greek tragedy.

Wright built Taliesin Two on the ashes of Taliesin One and developed even further his defensive style. For The Imperial Hotel in Japan he produced not only a *regional* ornament and style, related to the intricate brackets of Japan, but quite the most complicated set of horizontal battlements one can imagine. They suggest the elaborate Imperial terraces of Japan or China—specifically the white gnarled balustrades of the Forbidden City—that opened tier upon tier, as solid and imposing as the Emperor's edict. Partly they develop from the horizontals of the Prairie School and Midway Gardens. The latter was one of the most fantastic public schemes Wright ever built. Run up in the amazing time of just ninety days, it was built by a team that included artists, painters, muralists, sculptors and decorators—all under the control of a unifying idea, and impressario, Wright himself.[27] Here was the integrated 'cathedral to everyday life', dedicated to drinking beer and listening to music—a German *beergarten* with two orchestras, one for high- and one for low-brow, Mozart and dancing. Again the eclecticism is out in the open with the plan resembling a Chinese palace, the finials resembling Secessionist decoration, the neon like the illuminated signs of the Futurists—ideas he picked up in his travels to Europe and the Far East. (I found a China guidebook in the Oak Park bookshelves—and Wright appears to have studied that country almost as much as Japan.)

Other such frenetic, ornamental bastions were built over the next ten years while Wright was tying himself into ever more complicated conjugal knots. This sad, if strange and exotic story is long and

Midway Gardens, Chicago, 1913-14, destroyed 1929. An exuberant, vulgar and populist beer garden with music, and many redeeming virtues, such as an extensive sculpture programme carried out, for the most part, by Alfonzo Iannelli. The plan stretches a whole block and has an ingenious set of interlocking tiers. Note the patterned concrete block, an early use. (Photo: F. R. Yerbury)

Taliesin III, 1925 and later. The dining room, a larger space today at Olgivanna's insistence, has as usual small inglenooks next to it, and also fragments of Oriental pottery, built into the walls.

involved, and it has already been well told by Robert C. Twombly in his book *Frank Lloyd Wright, His Life and His Architecture* (re-edited 1979).[28] There's no need to analyse this period, since it produced little in the way of work, and that, as already said, was based on defensiveness, grief and constant movement. Suffice it to say that he became involved with a tempestuous adventuress and part-time sculptress, Miriam Noel; their living arrangement necessitated more press conferences justifying an illicit love; and she gave him such a rough time that, in an act of extreme desperation, he decided to marry her.

Where would a romantic choose to hold this wedding? On a Wisconsin bridge, in the wilderness, in a secret midnight ceremony, surrounded only by a friend to administer the service and the muttering bullfrogs. So private, for a change, was this act that when Miriam Noel later called a press conference to reveal her divorce plans, the greatest news was that they had been married in the first place!

Tragedy followed tragedy. Taliesin Two was burned, and during the fire neighbours not only helped douse the flames, but helped themselves to some of Wright's oriental art as well. Wright has described this 'fight with Isaiah' in his autobiography:

'No, fight the fire. Fight! Fight, I tell you! . . . I was up in the smoking roof, feet burned, lungs seared, hair and eyebrows gone, thunder rolling as the lightning flashed over the lurid scene, the hilltop long since profaned by crowds of spectators standing silent there. I stood up there and fought. Isaiah? . . . Were they the 'force' that had struck again? Were they really 'Isaiah'?[29]

The storm broke, rain saved part of Taliesin, and the calcined fragments of Tang heads, and the Oriental pottery that remained, were absorbed into the masonry walls of Taliesin Three, where they remain today. This characteristic Wrightian space, which has both large and small places together, still conveys a sense of the horrors it has witnessed. Is it the brooding darkness of the pitched ceiling set off against the horizontal glare of light?

The only piece of luck that occurred for this ill-fated man was that Miriam Noel walked out on him, and he then met, quite by chance, the woman who was to rescue him from further self-destruction: Olgivanna Milanoff, an Eastern European aristocrat and something of a romantic herself. They met in Chicago in 1924, at a performance of the Petrograd Ballet. Wright dramatises the afternoon encounter as an extraordinary coincidence, since there was only one empty seat left in the crowded hall, right next to his painter friend Jerry Blum, and right in their own box. As he tells it Jerry Blum made overtures to this 'Russian aristocrat', which so angered him that he would have thrown the painter over the edge, except he would hurt too many people below. Then Wright and Olgivanna exchanged silent looks. 'The glance went home: a strange elation stole over me. Suddenly in my unhappy state of heart, lonely for one thing, something cleared up— what had been the matter with me came to me in the face—it was, simply, too much passion without poetry. Starved . . . for poetry . . . that was it.'[30] If at fifty-seven he was 'starved for poetry', then at twenty-six she too was suffering from an unhapppy marriage and, further coincidence, to an architect. They were natural partners, and the way she described their meeting to me coincided with his account:

Olgivanna Milanoff Wright about the time of their marriage. (Photo: State Historical Society of Wisconsin)

> When I first met him it was very strange. We were in a box and you see I was late and had to rush very fast to get to—of all things—the Russian ballet. An usher escorted me to a box and next to a man I had seen walking in the foyer: he had a marvellous head of hair and a very rich and lovely, distinguished, beautiful face. He looked at me and then turned back to the ballet and then looked again. He had a friend who was bolder who said—'I want you to meet Frank Lloyd Wright, he is my friend'. I answered 'I have never heard of him before'. 'What, you didn't hear of Frank Lloyd Wright?'

By tea time, at the Congress hotel after the ballet, he was, once again, totally in love:

We danced in a very small space and sat down and he talked to me about his life, about the misfortunes, about the burglaries, the horrors and everything he had to go through. He amazingly told me *everything*, as though, as he said, he had known me all of his life.

The misfortunes that Wright recounted didn't stop there. Indeed, the unfortunate Miriam Noel, now inflamed by his new love, pressured him with police writs, law suits and federal agents for the next four years. After hiding for a month, with Olgivanna and their daughter Iovanna, the three were discovered by the police and had to spend humiliating night in jail.

In spite of all the trouble, several important things emerged from this chronicle of disasters: first in Olgivanna, he found the romantic attachment that could help, not destroy him; secondly, he started work on that mammoth job of introspection, *An Autobiography*, which was to result in his new self-assessment as the struggling and sometimes persecuted architect; lastly he combined the bastion style, in several western houses, with a new romantic manner evolved from California.

Perhaps Wright's most extraordinary client at the time was Mrs Aline Barnsdall, an oil baroness who wanted to build an avant-garde theatre complex right in the centre of the movie world—Los Angeles. She, like Wright at the time, was forever on a train or boat, collecting exotic ideas as she moved.

Wright designed several romantic schemes for her over the years (one had teepees), but they all had horizontal platforms extending over the top of a hill—'Olive Hill' it was called, because of the olive trees. Her favourite flower was the hollyhock, and it's a mark of Wright's sympathies and balanced theory that he could accept his client's taste and translate this plant into one of the great architectural metaphors; it unifies the house. The hollyhock is everywhere, and everywhere stylised in ornamental patterns so that it can emerge as clues to a hidden secret.

Wright speaks about an 'integral ornament' here, which has combined with the streamline and a mathematical rhythm. He allows that 'conscience troubled me a little'. That 'voice within' said 'what about the machine crying for recognition as the normal tool of your age?'[31] But, he answers, the 'Californian romance' a 'bit sentimental withal', still has its integral ornament; a mark not only of rhythmical integrity, but thematic unity as well.

We see hollyhock soldiers guarding the top of the outdoor platforms, and they transform themselves into Indian women sitting either side of the grand stairs. The image is both abstract enough to be part of the rectilinear masses and specific enough to be a flower and woman. On the inside of the building the flower is stylised again and used as

Wright, Olga Married On Western Ranch

Marries Dancer On Same Day That Divorce Went Into Effect

BULLETIN

The Bank of Wisconsin obtained a deficiency judgment amounting to $10,839.60 against Frank Lloyd Wright today. The judgment order was issued by Judge A. C. Hoppmann in circuit court here. Issuance of the judgment was ordered by the court because the bank, which held a mortgage judgment of approximately $40,000 against the estate of Taliesen, at Spring Green, failed to obtain that amount when the estate was sold several weeks ago.

Frank Lloyd Wright, internationally known for the turbulence of his domestic affairs as well as for his achievements in architecture, Saturday in California received both a final decree of divorce and a marriage license. He married Mme. Olga Milanoff at Rancho Sante Fe, a suburb of San Diego, on the same date that his divorce from Mrs. Miriam Noel Wright became final.

Formal announcement of the ceremony was made by telegraph Sunday to friends in Chicago, as follows:

"Married Aug. 25 at Rancho Sante Fe, by the Rev. Charles Knight of La Jolla, Olga Ivanhovna, daughter of Ivan Lazovich and Militza Milanoff, Cetinje, Montenegro, to Frank Lloyd Wright, son of Anna Lloyd Jones and William Cary Wright, Taliesin, Wis. We are altogether well and happy, going to put new life into new buildings in the great Arizona desert spaces during the next year or two.

"FRANK LLOYD WRIGHT."

Ends Troubles in Courts

This most recent chapter in the marital experiences of the architect marks the culmination of hostilities between himself and his former wife, Mrs. Miriam Noel Wright, begun three years ago. It was at that time that he first

(Continued on page 4)

Wright, Olga Are Married In California

(Continued from Page One) attempted to get his freedom from his second wife, for the announced purpose of legitimatizing his relations with Mme. Milanoff, who was about to become the mother of his child.

In this endeavor he was repeatedly repulsed by Miriam Noel Wright, who persisted in refusals to give him a divorce until one year ago, when a settlement was effected. Six weeks ago Mrs. Wright entered the bungalow occupied by Wright and Mme. Milanoff in La Jolla, smashing $3,000 worth of furniture with an ax.

Baby Iovanna, the child born to Mme. Milanoff in a Chicago hospital is now two years and eight months old. She has a stepsister, Svetlana, 12, who is the daughter of Mme. Milanoff by a former marriage to Vladimir Hinzenberg of Chicago, from whom she was divorced.

Taliesen, the home designed and built by Wright at Spring Green, Wis., was sold under the hammer on July 30, for $25,000, to satisfy a mortgage. It was at one time the scene of his romance with Mamah Borthwick Cheney, who with her two children was killed there by an insane Negro butler. Later Mrs. Miriam Noel Wright occuuied it with him.

Say Charges To Be Dropped

SAN DIEGO, Calif. — (AP) — Frank Lloyd Wright, who was married Saturday at Rancho Sante Fe to Olga Ivanova Milanoff, said he hoped to resume his profession without further interruption or notoriety. His wife was educated as a teacher and has followed that profession, although she frequently is referred to as a dancer, Wright said.

Nothing was known here of the whereabouts of Miariam Noel Wright, former wife of Wright, who recently appeared in San Diego and filed a statutory charge against Wright and the woman he married, on the ground that the year's limitation of divorce liberty had not expired.

Wright, Olga Wed

Frank Lloyd Wright

Olga Milanoff

Newspaper Headlines, Capitol Times, August 27, 1927.

Aline Barnsdall, Hollyhock House, Los Angeles, 1917-20. Outdoor platforms, like theatre seats, look over a central stage which never got its drama company. The hollyhock sentinels guard the roof, while they are stylised as finials to either side of the grand staircase; the vertical stem becomes the torso of an Indian woman, the flowers her square braids—the image is both abstract and figurative, mathematical and a woman. (Drawing: collection of Edmund Teske)

dining chairs so that their high backs become vertical skyscrapers (in fact they may have led to his later tall buildings). Over the fireplace, as always the centre of family life, Wright has turned the hollyhock into a portrait of Mrs Barnsdall on her drag-racer—the image of a footloose American. He has dramatised this with light from above, diffused through art glass, and the four elements below: Earth, Air, Water and Fire (one has to cross a mini-moat to reach the fireplace)[32]. Of course this is just an interpretation of the abstraction, and it could represent mathematical and musical harmonies in form, as others have argued. Yet if we keep in mind that Wright often referred to Mrs Barnsdall's

Barnsdall Fireplace. The central hearth with its abstract representation of Mrs Barnsdall (?) also expresses the four elements and dramatises light. Only the motto over the fireplace is missing.

'restless spirit', that he used the hollyhock to represent three or four different hidden meanings, then the interpretation is not too fanciful.

The virtue of abstract representation is its suggestiveness, its ability to fit in with abstract rhythms and geometries and still images without naming them. Used in this way Wright's 'integral ornament' has a creative power to provoke the imagination and stimulate various interpretations. It's of interest that later, municipal designers, not usually known for their imagination, have further transformed the hollyhock so now the house is surrounded by very sympathetic, metal lighting fixtures—also representing the plant. And historians, as well

Hollyhock House entrance left, living room above pond, right. The forms seem Mayan and concrete, but actually a lot of the construction is inexpensive California vernacular: stud walls and stucco. This 'California Romanza' seems like a movie set awaiting hordes of centurions to guard its battlements, yet ironically the form was intended to shelter an amateur theatre.

as the general public, have continued to see a host of exotic images in this house, including large, Mayan temples, leaning their massive walls inward to symbolise an earth-like stability. So Wright has used abstract representation in a very powerful way, and at a time when Modernists were denying ornament, to point up both general and particular meanings: the landscape, the Olive Hill, the four elements, and then Mrs Barnsdall the 'restless spirit', Indian ancestors of the site, and rootedness.

The 'Californian Romance' which really drives its roots into a hill is the Ennis House. It occupies the end ridge of a mountain range like a squat, massive fortress with tiny slit windows. It turns a boxy back to the street and tilts its defensive walls—against the imaginative eyes of the Hollywood Press? Perhaps not; its owner was not being arrested in 1924, as Wright was, for violation of the Mann Act. Nevertheless, everything speaks of solidity, stability, mass, as if Wright was trying to compensate for his own restless existence on the run.

It's also part of an architectural breakthrough—this and the other 'textile-block' houses—an attempt to invent a regional form of mass-production suitable to the South-West. It is partly based on Indian symbolism, Mexican-Mayan symbolism and even reinforced concrete. And the Mayan design has actually been taken up nearby, in a local cinema in downtown Los Angeles, so the regional language has taken root in at least one popular building type, even if it hasn't led to the local, Californian dialect that Wright wished to create. Like the Prairie Houses twenty years previously, there is a dramatic spatial procession through small and large places, taking one down and up steps, through tight and wide apertures, until one reaches the culmination—the dining table, here combined with the other focus, the hearth. The spatial and lighting contrasts which articulate this procession make it

Charles Ennis House, Los Angeles, 1923-4. White canted forms crown the hill with a concrete 'hill', like a pyramid, ziggurat or a Mayan platform, the sign of hill. The squat proportions—always criticised since the Larkin Building—are exaggerated so far in linear directions as to become something else; a base, a plinth, for inhabitation. Note the repetitive direction of the textile block, used as an ornamental border, wandering line or texture.

Ennis House textile blocks are used sometimes in mirror-symmetry around a lighting fixture. The design has an L-shape, stepped diagonally in a series of positive and negative echelons, so it's both complete (as a square) and open (as a diagonal).

Ennis House hearth. The Chinese Cloud pattern, stylised at the front gates, has now been transformed into a concrete block, and finally, a figurative element, the Indian symbols for fire. Note the inglenook of space as high as the chimney-piece, and lower than the dining space. Again low next to high.

into one of the great set-pieces for an architectural promenade. If one starts at the front gate, with its stylised Chinese cloud patterns, and walks quickly to the culmination, ducking where necessary to avoid the low ceilings, the surprising contrasts can be very much like explosions of light and space, perhaps because they are given the most extreme opposites; darkness and mass. Wright, like Beethoven, accentuates drama through violent contrast.

Because of the ornament, and historical imagery, Philip Johnson a few years later, ridiculed Wright, as 'the greatest architect of the *nineteenth* century'. But it wasn't only those aspects of architecture Wright was keeping alive in the romantic houses: there was also metaphor and simile, the way architecture can suggest images outside its own realm. 'Fallingwater', 1936, perhaps his most famous image, was like 'The Hollyhock', designed around a name that could summarise the intention.

This intention was conceived from the view below a waterfall, as several of Wright's perspectives show, so that the white cantilevers have maximum contrast with the dark green woods and dark shadows they cast. Again the contrasts could be called Beethovian. More to the point, the name 'Fallingwater' is taken up by these frozen, concrete horizontals: 'Stillwater' they could be called, because they take the white sheets of foam, evident as white planes in Wright's drawings, and turn them into architectural equivalents, metaphors of still, frozen water. It's stretching the metaphor, but they can even be seen as imaginary diving boards, from which one leans out and mentally jumps into the cool bubbling water below. They are in maximum contrast with the stone verticals, metaphors for solid rock, which in fact *do* tie the building to the rock.

White equals moving water and the exciting instability of a cantilevered terrace, while brown equals stability, structure and permanence. The two are in such extreme opposition that the drama takes our mind off what is missing from the usual house: no roof, no base, no discernible heirarchy and front door. Just horizontal pools, slabs, pergola and courses of stone, all sliding past each other. It's a performance worthy of De Stijl, of Van Doesburg and other Dutch abstractionists, whose sliding planes themselves derived from the Prairie Houses. And yet clearly Wright is showing the Modernists they can have their abstract planes and language, with metaphors and even a primitive, organic ornament. The philosophy is not exclusivist, but catholic, reconciling opposites, in the *spirit* of tradition.

❈❈❈

Fallingwater. The overlapping planes sliding in opposite directions of De Stijl, but with a Japanese attention to water and nature, and the continual interest in metaphor and ornament. (Photo: US Information Service)

Edgar J. Kaufmann Residence, Fallingwater, Ohiopyle, Pennsylvania, 1935-6. The cantilever principle of reinforced concrete finally interpreted as a metaphor, of slabs of still water over rushing, noisy, falling water below. Dark and light, architecture and nature, are in maximum contrast. (Photo: Robin Lough)

WHILE WRIGHT WAS DESIGNING EXTRAVAGANT METAPHORS FOR millionaires trying to escape from the city, he was also trying to build inexpensive houses for the poor, in such a way as they might escape the city too. During the Depression, he changed his style and image yet again, leaving 'Wright the outcast romantic' for his new role as 'Wright, the grand, social visionary'. In the late twenties he became as respectable as he had been at the turn of the century. He gave countless lectures at major universities, started his Taliesin Fellowship—a visionary social workshop in itself—and in his mid-sixties adopted the persona of the quick-witted social sage. He wished to supply an impoverished America (and impoverished self for that matter) with an answer to Marxist revolution. This he called by the metaphor *Broadacre City*—a paradox, because it was *broad*, spread out like Los Angeles suburbia, and yet meant to be *urbane*, a city operating through quick transportation and communications. It would also give back Americans one acre to live on and farm (self-help was a keynote of Wright's economic theory, and Taliesin).

Broadacre city was presented to the world in model form in March 1935, ironically right in the heart of monopoly capitalism, and the densest urban congestion around—New York's Rockefeller Center. The new city was to be New York reversed, spread out to the point that it would be 'everywhere and nowhere', thus overcoming, as Marxism demanded, the contradiction between city and country. Partly this contradiction would be overcome by the new communication techniques—telephone, radio, later tv—the new light industries, and home industry. Also the fact that it is easier, given the new truck transport, to move things than people.

Superficially, Broadacres resembled the 'back-to-the-farm' movements of the Depression, and indeed today's urban sprawl, but there were significant differences. A family, the ultimate economic unit, was to have control of one acre to supply their minimal eating habits, and were to build their house, largely by themselves, from easy-to-assemble prefabricated parts. Wright believed the answer to economic breakdown was self-sufficiency, home produce and decentralised industry. The basic home for Broadacres was the 'Usonian House'—Usonian because it was to be very USA, very nationalistic, and something you could build yourself for $5,000. A cantilevered example, lacking its farmyard, but with very compact rooms slung along a brick wall and organised to the site and view—characteristic features—is the George Sturges Home in Los Angeles. Enigmatic, apparently windowless (they are protected behind the balcony), with very low ceilings and tight spaces that flow together, it makes an expressive fact out of cheap construction. Some may find it awkward

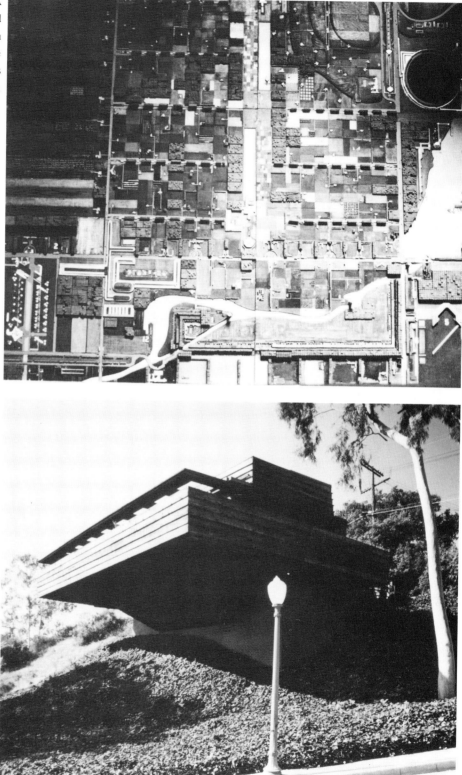

Broadacre City, Spring Green, model 1935+. A transportation grid with dead-end streets and greenbelts of one-acre plots, is interlaced with spread out city functions and tall offices. The patchwork quilt of activities at such scale was later to be realised in suburbanized America in the sixties.

George D. Sturges House, Brentwood Heights, Los Angeles, 1939. Cantilevered wood siding in horizontal bands, above a massive brick base, give this an aggressive tank-like appearance, a style later to emerge in America in the sixties. The windows are behind the jutting balcony.

and aggressive, like the formalism of the sixties which it has perhaps influenced, but it's still quite a feat given the small budget: a lonely ship ploughing through the ivy and eucalyptus of upper class Brentwood Heights.

Although Wright believed in capitalism, he thought that the land, the means of production and social credit—capital itself—should be distributed, not concentrated into monopolies. 'Little farms, little homes for industry, little schools, a little university and little laboratories' was the way one American Marxist characterised the decentralisation[33]. 'Small is beautiful' was to become a later slogan for many of the same ideas, including 'appropriate technology'. Suffice it to say that Wright was promoting Jeffersonian ideas of agrarian democracy and freedom, the *spirit* of tradition as he saw it in 1935, and if these ideas have been co-opted by a consumer society and turned into the worst excesses of suburbia they are, nonetheless, its hopeful signs.

In addition to this, Wright's architecture gained stature precisely because he had a social vision, a socially realistic ideal towards which he could shape his buildings. This gave his architecture an intention and symbolism it would otherwise have lacked, and also brought him into contact with clients who shared an idealism. While *Broadacre City* was never built, except in fragments (isolated Wrightian monuments or houses), the Johnson Wax Administration Building, an interesting social experiment, was completed. It had so many social amenities, such as an attractive cafeteria, and squash courts—and still *is* such an enjoyable place to work—that people have actually been queueing up to work since it opened in 1936.

Like the Larkin Building of 1904 the image of a company cathedral has been carried out in every detail and piece of furniture: from the outside pyrex tubing, whirling around bending curves to ease the driver into the carport, to the streamlines down the clerestory windows—it's all in motion. Everyone arrives by car and swings around streamlines made thinner by the plastic tubes. Even the 'mushroom columns' seem to spin and make the dreaded parking lot into a delight of 'lily-pads' (as they were also called).

The entry to the nine-to-five routine is through golden, revolving cylinders—church doors that transform monotony—and they lead up to the first surprise: a leap of space three storeys to the narthex of the church. What Wright called his 'cathedral to work' then reveals its next great surprise, something we are unprepared for given the windowless exterior: that is the grand, broad nave of work space, with diffused light dancing overhead, and coming in as shafts of brightness from the edges, or bouncing in under the aisles. This is undoubtedly Wright's most convincing public space, the very thing that architecture

S. C. Johnson Administration Building, 1936, and *Research Tower*, 1944, Racine, Wisconsin. Horizontal streamlines of brick, stone and tube whip the driver around curves and into the covered parking areas. The monuments turn their back to what Wright called 'an utterly unworthy environment.'

Johnson Wax. Entrance narthex with revolving doors in polished brass and tubes to the right, gardens and sculpture hanging overhead.

Johnson Wax. Main nave with five aisles: the triumph of light and space, the American public realm, so much more authentic than later Regency Hyatts. Note the columns tapering downwards in the Cretan manner, and their neckings and lily-pad capitals. (Photo: US Information Service)

Bridge connecting-link to tower triples the pyrex arch through its reflective floor and sides. The detailing and materials are of a much higher standard than later Wright buildings.

View down pyrex tubes which Giedion celebrated for its space-time effects, is a drama of repetition and perspective. Executive offices look over main floor to right.

celebrates, the *res publica*. Wright said: 'The Johnson people have a profit-sharing system with their employees and when they got into that building one of the first consequences was tea in the afternoon. And their people didn't like to go home. They loved to stay in the building, be there, come early, enjoy it . . . .'[34] Of how many workplaces can this be said?

Social and architectural imagination come together in the inverted columns of the central nave space: they are, once again, a mixed metaphor becoming not only the aforementioned 'mushrooms' and 'lily-pads', which employees see, but also 'golf tees', and 'umbrellas' with little neckings, 'legs on tip-toes' and 'flying saucers' overhead. With the flickering light, mottled by the tubes, and turning a bluish-green tint, it creates the impression that a busy race of aquatic worker-fish are darting to and fro in a giant bowl. In this grand space everyone mixes—secretaries, lawyers, managers, scientists, mid-level executives trying to find new markets for wax polish or, more likely today, their new synthetic products which are aimed at killing off the world's bugs and mosquitoes. It's the ultimate nerve-centre for a multinational which is still privately owned. One can criticise the religion of work, and corporate conformity, but in this cathedral of business Wright has made everyday commerce into a pleasure and ritual. The Protestant work ethic has finally been sanctified: no strikes, no unions, and lots of amazing details to ponder when you're mad at the boss.

***

LIFE MAGAZINE, STRETCHING ITSELF FOR A SUITABLE METAPHOR, described this building as looking 'like a woman swimming naked in a stream', a simile Wright quoted approvingly. The front page articles, he said, were worth two million dollars of advertisement. On January 17th 1938 Wright appeared on the cover of *Time* magazine; later it would be a two cent stamp. After his early experience with the yellow press, and then his success as the respectable architect, in the thirties, he started to realise the emergent rules of a commercial society, the one that was nurturing Mr. and Mrs. Ronald Reagan for their future, starring roles. One way to get commissions in a consumer culture is to dominate the media, and nothing appeals to them more than sensation. So 'Wright the sensationalist' was the last of his four characters to emerge after the Second World War. From this date to his death in 1959 he spent as much time giving interviews, and being a celebrity, as in designing buildings. In the age of media stars—radio, film, soon tv—Wright mastered them all, and instinctively helped create the system with which we are still saddled: the 'star system of architectural heroes', the one which Michael Graves, Norman Foster and a few others very much dominate.

Wright on a USA 2 cent stamp.

By 1950 Wright's sure instinct for promotion had paid off professionally. Instead of the meagre one or two commissions per year which he got in the twenties and which is still the lot today of good architects, he received an extraordinary thirty-eight—and this for a man who was eighty-three!

But the media attention, the time, energy and personal involvement it demanded, executed their revenge. Most of the buildings produced in these years betray an excessive vulgarity, or overruling ambition, which the young Wright would have called 'grandomania', and most people today call kitsch. Sometimes it's successful, sometimes not. The Grady Gammage Auditorium in Tempe, Arizona, finished after his death, is in what could be called the Late Hoola-Hoop Style, crossed with the Lollipop Manner. Columns look exactly like what they aren't: ruched curtains pulled back for the opening of an opera. Perhaps on certain evenings, when there's a strong, pink Arizona sunset, these Pop symbols can look amusing and even appropriate. But holding up what now looks like a hat box, they seem more embarrassed than enjoying themselves.

Overstatement was as much in Wright's pronouncements as it was in the over-ripe style of these later buildings. In the thirties he had said in jest: 'I warn Henry-Russell Hitchcock right here and now that, having a good start, not only do I fully intend to be the greatest architect who has yet lived, but the greatest who will ever live'. Perhaps in the fifties he started believing it. Whatever the reason—age, arrogance, public-

Grady Gammage Auditorium, Tempe, Arizona, 1959-62. Thin concrete columns rise sixty feet to hold what looks like a hat box. On the ramps are light sconces held together by hoola-hoops. Note the ruched curtain capitals in concrete. (Photo: Robin Lough)

ity, volume of work—there is a falling off in quality that asks to b explained.

The Greek Orthodox Church in Wauwatosa, produced when Wrigh was eighty-nine years old, shows both his strengths and weaknesses a this stage. Unlike a Modernist church it makes allusions to traditiona models and motifs. Its interior gold dome recalls Santa Sophia in Istanbul, but floats its flatter shape above small circular windows in an unexpected way. There are many refreshing innovations with tradi tion: for instance, the Greek cross plan interacts with the four pier and bowl shape in a way that recalls a planter Wright designed fo himself circa 1906. Curve and counter-curve, and then repeatec flattened arches, play off against each other in syncopation. On ar abstract level this is just the kind of organic architecture for which Wright fought.

However, as we move closer and look at more specific elements doubts begin to grow. The images which seemed to be abstract take or horribly concrete associations: those back-to-back curves now ma produce the image of a flying saucer, with a spiky crown of thorns descended on an upturned fruit bowl. Details are worked out with the precision of a blind engineer; arches collide with piers, just at thei weak points. The syncopation one so admires, could it simply resul from the non-ordering of the round motifs? Once those doubts anc images are planted they lead to further wild speculations, association of the most bizarre kind. Is the dome a giant blue hamburger, does i relate to the nearby, blue Wauwatosa water tank? Or is this really flying saucer with the prickly fringe on the top? Surreal metaphor may add an interest to the building, but they do so at the expense o our taking them, or it, veey seriously. In the case of Bruce Goff, who was very influenced by Wright, this surrealism was more intentional just as the kitsch was heartfelt and exuberant. With Wright, however it seems to result from a lack of control. Certainly no critic or historiar has yet seen fit to admit and defend it.

In other late-Wright buildings his 'honest arrogance', which he preferred to 'false humility', can, paradoxically, produce modesty of a sort. The interior of the Marin Civic Center quite intentionally does away with the image of a pompous, governmental center. It substitutes the form of a shopping centre for that of the authoritarian, classical temple, the older convention for this building type. Michael Graves and I debated this imagery and its appropriateness:

CJ: Michael, obviously Wright was trying to humanise the bureaucra cy and give an image to a civic centre that wasn't overpowering: so he's made this space into a kind of greenhouse shopping centre with a drag strip below, as you can hear. The citizen was meant to feel at ease here

Wrightian planter, Oak Park, circa 1912. Often Wright, like Le Corbusier, would remember an earlier design idea and transform its size and function later in life.

Greek Orthodox Church, Wauwatosa, Wisconsin, 1956-8. Interior gold dome towers above an array of jewel-like windows, reminiscent of Santa Sophia, but the Byzantine idea in a new key, with a new material. The decoration, stained glass and lighting fixtures are admirable in intention and most unfortunate in execution. Their kitsch, notional quality shows none of the care and thought that Wright put in his details in the early 1900s.

Greek Orthodox Church, exterior. Arches collide into piers and the syncopation of all the round curves does not seem to work out into complex rhythms, but rather be random. The general volumetric and spatial idea is, however, ingenious. If only Wright had worked this ingenuity into the details.

and enjoy himself. Do you think that's a fitting image for a civic centre?

MG: Well, certainly part of it is. Wright was trying to get round the problem of city government being all powerful and attempting to get us to participate in it. You can walk into these offices here and shop for services.

CJ: Don't you think it lacks ceremonial quality then?

MG: Well, it never had a centre, because that's what the linear idea is about. It's a diagram.

CJ: It lacks ceremony; it has nothing that elevates government in any metaphorical sense. It remains a shopping centre, or mall, in its imagery.

MG: A utilitarian rather than memorialising building.

CJ: And all this anodised aluminium everywhere, down below, over our heads, that's imitating gold. That contradicts Wright's early principle 'in the nature of materials'.

MG: Well, I don't know. I have no problem with gold: think of the Aztecs usage, and the interest Wright had in that kind of decoration. It might give us a sense of inspiration, the idea of preciousness . . . although this is indeed false preciousness.

CJ: So in a way this doesn't humanise the building any more than do the long corridors . . . .

MG: Well, I have no problem with the Tuscan Red on the floor.

CJ: That's Tuscan?

MG: Well it borders on something . . . .

CJ: I'd say it's Municipal Red.

MG: I think it's trying to be earthen-like, trying to root the building in the ground.

CJ: He's made the dome blue.

MG: He's trying to use colour naturalistically.

CJ: Actually the colours aren't too far from your Portland Building. Is that where you picked them up?

MG: (Laughs) Oh no.

This building contradicts many of the principles Wright fought for as a youth: 'integral ornament'? It drips off the sides into golden baubles. There are so many circles repeated here one can say he was suffering from circlemania. In favour of marrying site and building? It is not *of* the two hills it sits rather heavily *on*. Against elite government? Here only car drivers can influence city hall. Against phoney structure and applied historical imagery? Here the tiered arch form, borrowed from great Roman aqueducts, actually hang in tension. All fifty-one definitions of organic architecture cancelled, defied. As a serious building it fails, and yet this failure has not received criticism.

MG: Well, Americans, critics, many of them, have elevated Wright to the point where . . . .

CJ: He's uncriticisable?

MG: He's uncriticisable. He did good and bad buildings, but they elevate him to the point where almost everything is all right.

CJ: But Marin, on one level, has to be considered the epitome of kitsch. It's very sentimental and uses things in a phoney way. I think it's a *successful* example of kitsch, outrageously funny. In kitsch 'nothing succeeds like excess' and when you see this 560-foot Helena Rubenstein bowling alley behind me with its golden baubles dripping off the side . . . .

MG: No, I think it's personal kitsch in this case. Given Wright's age, the time he did it . . . .

CJ: You think it has to do with his age?

MG: I think like many artists he went a bit ga-ga in the last stage when his personal touch is not there. His studio had an enormous amount to do with this.

CJ: But a lot of artists, such as Titian, were producing great work at the end.

MG: A lot of artists like Picasso were not . . . .

It may well be that we are still too close to put this work in proper perspective, and that it will take a few defenders of Wright kitsch and Goff kitsch, the relation of this to different taste cultures, before we can get the balanced assessment right. In any case, in spite of his great age, Wright could still produce sensational architecture which was sensationally good (while still being flawed). The Guggenheim Muse-

Marin County Civic Center, Marin, California, 1957-61. Interior walls, 560 and 850 feet long, are given a flat, glazed arch rather like the great shopping arcades of the nineteenth century. Space is punctured through several levels.

Marin Civic Center. One wing shows the tension arches and baby-blue circles disappearing to a sublime infinity. As a Pop icon, as the ultimate one-liner on the highway, the image rates rather high. In what sense did Wright intend the Post-Modern commercial style that Venturi later proposed?

um, designed in 1943 finished in 1956, is one masterpiece in the circular style whose most obvious sin is to be more powerful, and often interesting, than the art exhibited inside it.

Wright talked about the *unity* of the form: no angles, or abrupt changes of shape.[35] Everything is made from one material, reinforced concrete, painted a single colour—creamy white. The shell-form, the structural continuity of a curved surface, pulls the variety of elements together into a single idea. The building is a round temple to art, with swelling horizontals that loom upwards and outwards at the top—the reverse of usual buildings and unlike a round Greek temple with its vertical order. It's a temple for New Yorkers to engage in one of their most religious of activities: going to an art opening, seeing themselves seeing art and its ever-rising economic fortunes.

MG: I think museums *should* be temples to art, but this seems to be more a temple to light. This incredible light comes through the dome and is finely filtered by the time it gets reflected back to the surfaces of the wall. It's a temple to light and procession, to be seen in rather than see paintings in.

CJ: Oh come on. You can see the art from afar, and have a sense of expectation when you approach it. You can see it from an angle, and of course up close when your expectation is rewarded.

MG: But all the walls are slanted back and the paintings are tilted.

CJ: Well, that's the great thing. It's a very kinetic experience to walk where nothing is flat. The floor is not only tilted down, but in, and the paintings are tilted back and the underneath of each floor is canted, so you feel like you are in a cyclotron, or mini-accelerator . . . .

MG: Yes, again, talking to you, I feel I'm a little old fashioned. I'd rather have a little stability in my life . . . especially when I'm looking at a picture.

CJ: You *can* have stability here. The cant is only 5 per cent, so you can stand straight. In any case, on a flat floor you always stand shifting on one foot. I'm not disturbed by the tilt, nor by the dramatic space that you can compare to a great sort of womb-like volume that swells up while these very masculine elements, such as the men's room, penetrate into the space. That kind of suppressed, sexual symbolism creates a great sense of release, if you like, which is enjoyable in a temple to art . . . .

MG: Too much, Charles, I think you've gone too far . . . .

But genius is knowing how far 'too far' you can go, and with the Guggenheim Museum, Wright has judged this distance with perfect accuracy. The building's feminine curves, which are desirable at this point in the city, are in judicious counterpoint with the monotonous, grid-iron of New York. And the sexual theme is never stated, or

Solomon Guggenheim Museum, New York, 1943-56-59. Swelling trays of space, like white ash trays, push out on Fifth Avenue to contrast with the darker, masculine grid of the city. This Pop icon, reduced in cues to a formal gestalt, can be miniaturised to a postage stamp and still have visual power. The way space and movement are defined on an urban level make this a monument, *the* temple for New Yorkers to observe one of their favourite rituals: the opening of a show, the economics of taste. The round, ziggurat form was first proposed by Wright in 1925 for a planetarium.

Guggenheim interior. Primitivist expression, the men's room, thrusts up to one side of the dome, while further sexual oppositions are also indicated at a very abstract level. The power of abstract representation is its coherent suggestion.

Guggenheim interior, with Scandinavian, Post-Modern art on display, 1982. Round trays allow not only people to be displayed dramatically, but works of art to be viewed from all sorts of angles, thus producing drama of a different kind.

(Photo: US Information Service)

explicit, so its undeniable presence is all the more intensely felt. One can fault the lack of ornament, the lack of certain scale and richness, but still applaud the inventive use of structure and space to suggest some themes which are never named. If one is going to design a monument—and a temple to art is surely that today—then one can use the most discontinuous form, the circle, in this perhaps oversimplified way. Alberti and Palladio recommended the circular form for Christian monuments, to stand out and above the rest of the city. So once again Wright is being very much in the spirit of tradition when he designs one of his most apparently novel forms.

✳✳✳

WRIGHT'S LIFE WAS A DRAMA IN FOUR ACTS. HE SOUGHT TO GIVE America a unique, democratic architecture and in the process became one of its most celebrated and autocratic leaders. He was the king: first of Oak Park Suburbia, then of dispossessed architects wandering in the Mid-West, then of social visionaries and finally of media celebrities. He was perhaps the greatest architect America has yet produced, certainly its most creative, but although he ruled the country with his influence, he never achieved the important governmental commissions. He never received the patronage of the state, church and establishment that, for instance, went to H. H. Richardson. This sad breakdown in culture, for that is what it is when the best go unrecognised or unused, was as much due to the architectural confusion within society as to Wright's arrogance. It may be for Michael Graves and current architects of skill to overcome the schisms which have developed within mass culture and its several elites. It takes willpower and power, as well as talent and conviction. Above all it takes an ability to draw visions of the good life, revive the perennial themes of architecture—of space, symbolism and art—in a new way. Wright had this rare power to draw, and draw on the spirit of tradition, so that in the end it supported his individual efforts, his particular 'truth against the world'.

THE RETURN TO THE PUBLIC REALM— MICHAEL GRAVES (1934-   )

ARCHITECTURE IS *THE* PUBLIC ART, THE ART OF THE PUBLIC REALM. This perennial truth was lost in Modern Architecture for two quite different reasons: because its language became abstract, esoteric, tied to a Machine Aesthetic and because the building tasks presented by society became more and more privatised, concerned with mass-housing and commercial functions. Clearly the architect can do little or nothing about the latter cause, but he is responsible for the former, the language of building. Here he makes choices which decide whether or not we have craftsmen, use artists in building, and produce an understandable, sensual environment. The story of Michael Graves, as it is of Post-Modern architecture in general, is the slow, often painful, account of the search for this new architecture. We haven't yet completed this synthetic language, but we *do* know the outline of its appearance.

Michael Graves was born, like Wright, in the Mid-West, Indianapolis, where the most public of institutions was not housed in a building but occurred outside, in the open flat-land; the 'Indianapolis 500', the car race. The polis devoted to the car, the destroyer of urbanity in its usual sense, makes Graves rather contemptuous of Broadacre City. His early life was spent in a spread out suburban sprawl which is the fate of many Americans: neither the pastoral landscape of a Capability Brown, nor the intensity of a city, nor the planned control of a garden city, but the compromised flatscape of commercial exploitation. 'There was nothing to love in terms of the real landscape', Graves said, 'and only a few public buildings of any note: Paul Cret's public library and a few monuments to the war dead. A good museum, where I drew on Saturday afternoon, and a symphony hall'. The heart of the city, such as it was in the nineteenth century, had been destroyed by the mass exodus of the middle class, and the relatively poor Graves family found itself stranded on the edge of the old boundaries which were now eroding.

Michael Graves in his wooden racer at eleven years. The 'Indianapolis 500' is one of the most public acts of this *polis*. (Photo: Graves)

Thomas Browning Graves and Erma Lowe Graves, circa 1970. (Photo: Graves)

Michael Graves' father came from an Eastern family that had moved West in search of new work in the livestock trade. This uncertain profession, bartering all day over the telephone to keep up with fluctuating prices, took its toll and the elder Graves turned to alcohol as a solace. His wife, a nurse, had to give up her profession after her two boys were born. Perhaps the instability led her to insist that Michael not become a painter. 'Unless you can draw like Picasso, you better become an engineer or architect.' So the young Graves was, like Wright, steered into the profession by his mother. But it was drawing that established his difference from other boys. Like them he did well at sports—'ran track, wrestled, played center at football, everyone in a Midwestern town plays sports'—but he didn't excel at school work, nor music.

MG: I did so poorly at playing the violin that it was finally taken away from me. The screech was too great for the house. But I wanted to excel in something, and everybody was brought out to do something when the guests came; so I was brought out to draw cartoons.

CJ: You were really brought out to draw as a performance? 'Here comes Michael drawing?'

MG: 'Here comes Michael drawing.' The neighbours would come over and sit around and Michael would draw in the middle of the living room floor.

A father who was often away from home, a dominant mother with a disability (she lost her leg through cancer), a Midwestern provinciality mitigated by the occasional contact with a cultural institution, relative poverty—the parallels with Wright are plain. Coincidentally the first book his mother gave him was on the drawings of Frank Lloyd Wright, and the first thing he did, when he got his driver's licence, was to drive all the way to Racine, Wisconsin, and visit the Johnson Wax Building.

MG: I was bowled over by it: the walls, all of those columns punctuating space like a hypostyle hall making space measurable, understandable, with a foreground, middleground and background. They divide up people, although I didn't realize it at the time, into various groupings. I wish more architects would look at it today because it takes architecture first, before spatial dissolvement, the open amorphous plan.

One should not overemphasise the parallels between Wright and Graves because there are as many differences, especially over the notion of organic architecture. Where Wright sought to unify architecture with nature—the site, its foliage as well as abstract rhythms—Graves seeks more urban contrast: the classical temple, or artefact, set in contrast with nature, in order to bring out the identity of each. Nonetheless, the parallels of background remain: both were country provincials who in moving to the city see its culture all the more clearly. Both seek to bring a ritualised center to family life around the hearth, or dining table. Both seek ritual in architecture. One of Graves' first acts as a teenager was to change religion, from being a Presbyterian to being Episcopalian.

MG: It was the first time I had really gone out on my own, at thirteen. What interested me about the Episcopalians was the ritual; the fact that I could participate in the ritual by helping with Communion as an acolyte.

CJ: Presbyterianism didn't offer enough ritual—like Modern architecture?

MG: Well, it was more a striking out on my own and becoming involved in a religion that was more *understandable.*

Graves fell in love at the early age of sixteen and married his high-school sweetheart Gail Devine when he was twenty-one. She was a painter and in this sense sympathetic to his impending career. He enrolled at eighteen in the Department of Architecture at the University of Cincinnati, and then pursued a rigorous academic life moving slowly, but surely, from one position to the next.

CJ: When you got to Harvard Graduate School of Design you followed the work of Le Corbusier?

MG: You either did or didn't. It was a pressure-cooker of a place, an experience I wouldn't want anybody to repeat.

CJ: After being pressure-cooked on Le Corbusier, and spending two years at the American Academy in Rome, you established yourself in Princeton doing late versions of Le Corbusier's work—white walls, abstraction.

MG: Le Corbusier's *Oeuvre Complète* was the one document, in eight volumes, that one could look to as a whole, like Palladio, Scamozzi or Letarouilly. All I had up to that time was styling, and superficial. I almost gave up architecture at the American Academy in Rome, because other disciplines seemed more defined. When I returned to teach at Princeton, with Peter Eisenman, he invited Colin Rowe to lecture. We'd been impressed by his articles—'The Mathematics of the Ideal Villa'— which compared Le Corbusier's work to Palladio's and made it understandable as a discipline.

CJ: So your early work, the Benaceraff House, is a Cubist collage of Le Corbusier's works, a collision of two of his ocean liners, with spikes and ship rails sticking out.

MG: I suppose mine *was* overly complicated . . .

CJ: I remember one of the great debates we had, at UCLA in 1976, was over the blue horizontal element—the balustrade—which you claimed was a column lying down, a blue Corbusier column which

Benacerraf House, Princeton, New Jersey, 1969. A Mannerist version of Le Corbusier's Villa Savoye with picture windows pushed towards the centre and structure pushed to the edge. The redundant use of structural elements to frame space, the strong use of colour and the emphasis on the curved 'celestial soffit' point to later concerns of Graves. But the Late-Modernist ones—the Machine Aesthetic, open space, primary colours—still predominate. The blue balustrade is also a Corbusier column lying on its side. (Photo: Laurin McCraken)

Benacerraf House, the 'celestial soffit' cutting up the sky into clouds, or imprinting a semantic dimension onto abstract syntax. From the earliest Graves had an interest in the conventional mythic nature of architecture: in his later work it just became more accessible, controlled and part of the whole building.

people would recognize.

MG: I remember joking about that, but I said it was *both* balustrade and column.

Our arguments were over the accessibility of architecture, how well it could communicate and to whom. Up to the middle seventies Graves was producing one ingenious intellectual exercise in Corbusian aesthetics after another. They were hard to follow for the layman, but for the afficianado, trained in Late-Modernist Scholasticism, they were the very stuff of architecture.

The Hanselmann House, back in Graves' home state of Indiana, brought the European aesthetic into the Mid-West forest, by a stream. Here was Le Corbusier's square box of a house, the Citrohan, but with one side bitten away on the diagonal to indicate the stairway. Ribbon windows were like Le Corbusier's except they were asymmetrically disposed. Double height volumes, extended entrance and central loggia were Corbusian. The white concrete volumes were Corbusian (although actually made in wood). The drawings were Corbusian. Their author could have been called Michael Corbusian: he could even counterfeit the master's signature. On the inside of the Hanselmann House, however, there was an indication of a different concern: the Corbusian mural introduces almost recognizable themes of the house, to aid in understanding its meaning. Here in a muted palette we can begin to see the green landscape, blue sky and pink earth or flesh, the

Hanselmann House, Fort Wayne, Indiana, 1967. A Mannerist play on Le Corbusier with concrete volumes made from wood, double squares rotated at forty-five degrees and stairways pulled at an exaggerated distance from the front door. (Photo: Tom Yee)

Hanselmann Mural identifies the diagonal composition and the way the landscape is to be seen. (Photo: Tom Yee)

conventions which were to become more explicit in later buildings. Sky, ground, nature, man—these are the fundamentalist themes you can understand, as long as there is a critic present with pointer in hand.

The strength and weakness of Graves' early work is that it is difficult to understand—cryptic, elitist, complicated—the very opposite of Wright's last, sensationalist work. In the early sixties American architecture was going through an inflationary expansion, a consumerist explosion based on oversimplified and aggressive forms, and the architecture of Graves, Eisenman and the 'New York Five' was directed against this banality. For the oversimplifications of the International Style, they substituted overcomplications; for the mindless bombast of a SOM Corporate headquarters, they substituted the most subtle commentaries on 'spatial layering', 'frontality and rotation', 'skews and ambiguity'. All these keywords were like the Mannerist's emphasis on *difficultà*, meant to change the 'too-easy' into the 'difficult to perceive', if not 'too-hard'[36]. Aesthetic experience demands effort on the part of the viewer; by definition its enemy is the cliché, the slogan, the one-liner.

In a period when Modern architecture was beginning to look like bad advertisements of good taste, Graves' Snyderman House is easy to understand; or at least understand the reasons for. All the Modernists' signs are taken to Baroque extremes of difficulty. The Corbusian grid is fragmented and left exposed, often carrying nothing but itself. Ribbon windows and punctured holes interplay in a slightly frenzied manner. Tiny cuts are made in stucco to indicate some obscure 'shear' of space that a PhD thesis will elucidate some day. Even Graves' programme notes, explaining the building, need reading twice: 'The "natural" is taken to mean that which shows the attributes of nature—irregularity, lyricism, movement. Similarly, "man-made" becomes synonymous with idealised form, geometry, stasis . . . Polychromy is used to refer to both natural and man-made elements'.[37] Eh? How can polychromy refer to *both*, especially since the 'idealised form', the grid, is white?

To ask such questions is to become involved in a long, tortuous and complicated debate as sophisticated in its distortions, blind alleys and suggested cues as the Snyderman House itself. We enjoy a labyrinth, and it's an ideal form for the personalised complications one wants in a house, but it leads to very dull, verbal analysis so I shall desist, and refer the interested reader to the monographs on Graves, or to the house itself.[38] The main point to be established is that the Snyderman House was the epitome of Late-Modernist complication, an aesthetic delight, but not an accessible, public architecture.

Graves had come to an impasse at the beginning of the seventies,

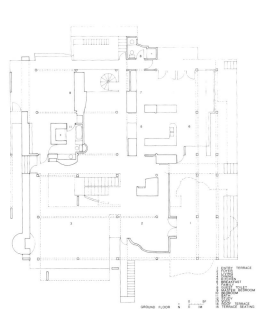

Snyderman House plan shows the two grid rhythms and then the walls and units placed in counterpoint to them.

Snyderman House, Fort Wayne, Indiana, 1972. An ideal white grid layers complex space in a regular rhythm (AABAA) while curved and punctured walls thread through this order: the former symbolise reason; the latter, nature. (Photos: Graves)

Alexander House, Princeton, New Jersey, 1971 and 1973. One of the additions to a house which led to Graves being known as the 'Cubist Kitchen King'. The celebration of landscape in the views and mural, and the emphasis on the hearth show emerging concerns. A cruciform of space around a central column implies a classical order within a Cubist composition. (Photos: Bill Maris)

both architecturally and on a personal level. It's true he was respected in academic circles. He was constantly publishing drawings and articles, had a job that would lead to a professorship at Princeton and had formed along with Eisenman and others the group known as the Whites, or The Five, because of the book *Five Architects*, published in 1972. This had opened up intellectual debate, something lacking in America, and led to other city groups forming: the 'Chicago Seven,' the 'Los Angeles Twelve', the 'Greys' and so on. But the doubt was beginning to grow just as it had in Wright after his first minor successes in Oak Park.

On an architectural level it was clear, as Charles Moore pointed out in his review of *Five Architects*, that the Late-Modernist work was inaccessible even to fellow-architects.[39] Secondly, as Graves mentioned to me, he was locked into small commissions.

MG: The kind of projects I had in those days were tiny: I was called the 'Cubist Kitchen King' and to do a kitchen or renovation you don't make any money. You get paid a pittance and hope you will get larger projects; instead you get more kitchens. And you know, kitchens beget kitchens, drawings beget more drawings and articles beget articles. It's a Catch 22: only big buildings beget big buildings. Somehow you've got to have luck, or whatever it is to get you over the hill.

Hustle, intellectual promotion combined with drawing skill? Whatever it would take, Graves did not have it in the early seventies, and throughout this decade he worked himself, almost blind, trying to get out of the kitchen.

MG: I think about my work all the time, and draw all the time. I'll come home exhausted after work and just think about the next deadline.

CJ: It makes being married to you difficult?

MG: It makes it impossible, you know; that's the greatest dilemma in my life. I want a family, I don't want to spend Christmas alone.

CJ: Apart from that there's the question of a change in approach, a change in style with a change in marriage and it strikes me that when you were married to Lucy, roughly between 1972 and 1977, there's a slight change in your architecture. With Wright you can see the influence of personal traumas, often in a very creative way. It's as if the change and growth in his architecture and personality is somehow connected with the change and growth in relation to women and the outside world. I'm not advocating polygamy; I'm trying to look for relationships between private life and public architecture.

MG: It's interesting you say that. One could make fun of the transfer of energy from one thing to another. But at the end of my relationship with Gail I was designing the Rockefeller House, one of my best buildings—a pity it wasn't built. I wasn't very much in our house, but always in the office, concentrating on that one building in very, very stressful times.

CJ: You transferred your stress into your work?

MG: I think so. That's a cliché, of course, but it's nevertheless what I did.

Michael and Gail had brought up two children during these years of incessant work; the late nights and gruelling life of an architect trying to make it to the top—the very ambitions which had undermined Wright's first marriage—took their toll. They ended up not man and wife, but brother and sister. Graves' second marriage to Lucy James, a dancer, lasted from 1972 to 1977 and during this period we can discern a slight shift in his work. Slowly, tentatively, more conventional elements are introduced into his repertoire: the emphasis on the hearth, window and door, the moulding used as a scaling device to divide up the wall, the voided keystone, the semantic use of colour. The painted murals take up these themes also.

A characteristic work is the Claghorn House Addition, yet another kitchen and porch added to a nineteenth-century building. This renovation uses fragments of conventional signs—the trellis which is an image of the garden—to suggest the condition to which many a suburban backyard aspires: that of a pastoral landscape. Blues, greens and red-browns carry forward the illusion: this is arcadia with a barbecue pit. Very subtle cues relate to the older Queen Anne House. One can just make out the pitch of the roof indicated by a one-inch void incised in the left pavilion. If one focuses very closely through the complicated layering, and conflicting Cubist cues, mouldings can be

Gail Graves, Paris, July 1965.

Claghorn Addition, Princeton, New Jersey, 1974-5. Another cruciform structure articulates space, while the colouring of traditional forms recalls customary associations: red for earth, blue for sky, green and trellis for landscape. The other signs—a voided keystone and one-half pitch—are very hard to discern.

Medical Office, Fort Wayne, Indiana, 1971. Enclosed rooms have mysterious spaces created—anything but antiseptic—that are punctuated by murals suggesting the landscape, water and sun. Rigid, functional, hospital space is thus humanised. (Photo: Graves)

discovered—'string coursing alluding to one's assumption of the floor as transposed ground plane'.[40] More helpful hints for the PhD industry.

It would all be slightly ridiculous were it not carried out with so much consistency and rigour. Countless drawings, of exquisite control, were turned out to make these backgrounds into walkthrough Cubist paintings. And the murals themselves give a presence and humanity so lacking in other buildings of the time. For instance Medical Offices built just previously have four or five murals located at nurses' stations or waiting areas, so that the anxious patients can be reminded of the landscape and focus on colourful objects which have very basic associations.

In fact anxiety and nervousness *can* be read into Graves' fragmented forms of this period. The conventional signs of disruption—the torn edge, the collision, the fragment—are present in much architecture of the seventies. Robert Venturi had written about the 'difficult whole' in the mid-sixties, and the notion of the unfinished building, the dissonant fragment, can be found in such diverse work as that of Lucien Kroll, SITE, Team Ten, James Stirling and Richard Meier. It became something of an orthodoxy, to symbolise an uncertain society. Colin Rowe had justified *Collage City* as a method of city planning, superior to holistic Modernism; Nathan Silver and I had written *Adhocism* for similar reasons. It would be surprising if Graves didn't have a frenetic compositional method.

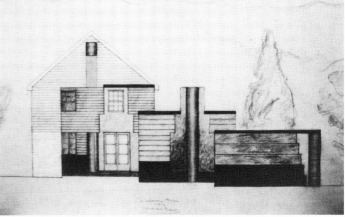

Schulman House, Princeton, 1976-7. An addition of a living room and garden wall accentuate the major parts in a calmer manner: front door is indicated by a keystone and the family hearth by a column. (Photos: Graves)

Yet by 1977 and the Schulman House Addition we can begin to see a simplification and consolidation of elements. The fragments of mouldings, columns, and colour are there, but they are less fussy. The painter has tried to cram less into his canvas. Green, red and blue now became more connected together, and relaxed, with the horizontal lines of the clapboard—which diminish in perspective. And the forms almost complete themselves: only a column top has jumped into the centre of the facade, to hang there, and the missing section of the cylinder is displaced to the right. There are several such jokes, but we can say a classical calm almost settles over the lot. Almost, but not quite.

During this period of consolidation Graves was obviously affected by the rise of Post-Modern architecture in different cities. Robert Stern and others in New York were becoming slightly more historicist in their use of forms. James Stirling and Leon Krier in London, Aldo Rossi in Italy and the Rationalists in many countries were all making use of archetypal shapes. There was no explicit use of ornament, nor classical elements beyond the most rudimentary, but these things were in the air. Also during these years Michael and I started to become friends, after his London exhibition with The Five in September 1975. We taught together in January 1976 at UCLA in Los Angeles and debated the public nature of architecture, how well it could be understood. One confrontation concerned his Benaceraff House, the obscurity of the blue balustrade as a column.[41] Another concerned the infamous hot dog stand in the shape of a hot dog, something that was too explicit for Graves. I favoured a more explicit use of metaphor in architecture and *The Language of Post-Modern Architecture*, 1977, was written to support the notion of a public, accessible language. Perhaps some of these arguments rubbed off on Michael, for by the end of the year he had crystallised a new style that was much more accessible,

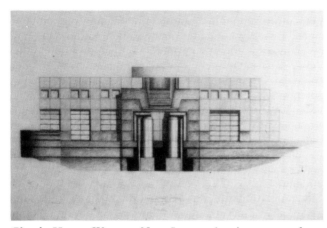
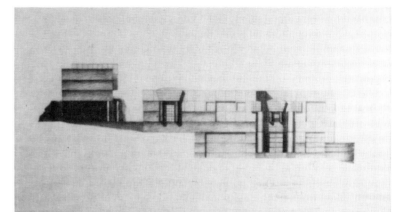

Plocek House, Warren, New Jersey, drawings 1978. Landscape and building interlock to form a whole. The approach by car up a steep hill is into an enclosed forecourt, like Raphael's Villa Madama. The 'voided keystone' cut out of the mass relates the building to the two main views and axes. The 'replaced keystone' will be built higher up the site as a studio. The first colour studies emphasise earth-like base, green sides and sky-blue columns. The final colours set a terra-cotta base against a cream top and blue-grey windows. (Photos: Proto Acme Photo)

calm and even, to a degree, conventional.[42] It was Post-Modern Classicism, and his designs for the Plocek House were the first in this manner.

Here for the first time in fifty years was a convincing synthesis of the important trends which had remained separate. Not since Le Corbusier crystallised the International Style in the 1920s, through the force of his painting and drawing too,[43] had such a masterful syncretic design occurred: it pulled together the Rationalist work of Krier and Rossi, so that fundamental shapes had their primal integrity. It gained from Venturian symbolism especially around the entrances: one could actually tell where the front door was, after being confused for so many years. Its collage, and *bricolage,* from Rowe and others, absorbed columns, keystones and elements of the landscape. It's tripartite ordering—foot, middle and head—were borrowed from the classical tradition; the plan from Raphael's *Villa Madama*, details from Edwin Lutyens. It was even the kind of Radical Eclecticism I was espousing because it used forms in a semantic way. Josef Hoffmann, the Pre-Modernist that interests Graves the most, was evident in the window grids. And yet all of this was, and is, a convincing new whole. Details are repeated around the building tying it together. The column appears by the ceremonial entrance as two piers, then as a central columnar stair, then as an end chimney—the focus of family space, the hearth. The keystone, and voided keystone, appear in elevation, plan and landscape. And as the drawings and Graves' words reveal, the composition includes the building *and* landscape as interdependent parts of a whole.[44]

Post-Modern Classicism was evolved in this and the Fargo-Moorhead project of the same time. Here we can see the classical language tied with the Modern—to produce the typical hybrid of Post-Modernism. Not a few critics mislabelled this as Neo-Classical, but the eclecticism, to say nothing of the epoch and technology, mark it

Plocek House, Warren, New Jersey, building 1979-82. The grid *appliqué*, an ordering device of Hoffmann and Wagner, is used to divide up the walls and windows at different scales. The layering of space around the ceremonial entrances accentuates the effect of transition, as does the voided keystone. The column is abstracted and then represented in several transformations including the chimney and central stair.

(Photos: Proto Acme Photo)

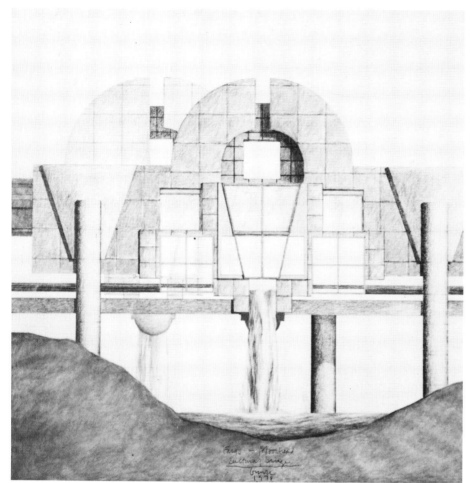

Fargo-Moorhead Cultural Center, Fargo North Dakota, Moorhead, Minnesota, 1977-8. The cultural bridge ties together two separate communities with its broken arch, window keystone, grid and symbolic waterfall in stone (an idea transformed from Ledoux). The Free Style Classicism can be seen in the tripartite elevation and anthropomorphic imagery. (Photos: Graves)

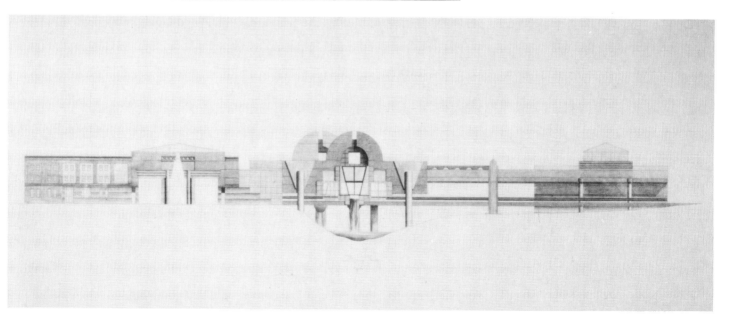

unmistakably of the present. Other Post-Modern Classical buildings of the same period were Charles Moore's Piazza D'Italia, 1976-9; Ricardo Bofill's Les Arcades du Lac, 1975, constructed 1977-80; Philip Johnson's AT&T, 1978, Arata Isozaki's Fujima Country Club, one of the first in the genre, 1973-4; most of the work of Hans Hollein, after 1975, Robert Stern and Robert Venturi, from the early seventies. Venturi claims credit for starting the movement, but it seems to me that Graves, with his ability to *synthesize through drawing,* really deserves credit for creating the hybrid style.[45] Venturian buildings tend to be studded, quite intentionally, with quotes, jokes and representational figures, whereas Graves' buildings, after 1977, are abstract representations of themes. The advantage of the latter is that the meanings are abstract enough to be generalised across a different range of tastes and interests, and yet still be recognisable enough to be understood.

Lucy Graves, Europe, summer 1970.

From 1978 onwards Michael Graves started being taken up by the national press, particularly *Newsweek* and the *New York Times.* He had already won considerable design awards, of *Progressive Architecture* and the local, New Jersey chapter of the A.I.A. A monograph was published in 1979 and his work started appearing regularly on the covers of design magazines. He was ready to emerge from the kitchen. But in spite of this publicity it didn't quite happen. Instead he went on selling his drawings, sometimes for several thousand dollars, and using the proceeds to keep his expanding office together. His relationship with Lucy had ended much as that with Gail had: too much time devoted to work, the acclaim that went to the architecture rather than the couple, the family. The jealousies of competition within the small world of architectural politics. None of this could lead to a satisfactory family life, so Lucy left him.

In 1979 he received his first large-scale, commercial break. Bobby Cadwallader, former president of the Knoll furniture company, wanted to inject new life into one he had just taken over, called Sunar. Cadwallader commissioned Graves to design temporary showrooms for Sunar in New York and Chicago. These were followed by more permanent ones in Los Angeles, Houston and Dallas, as well as the original two cities. In nearly every case the showrooms consisted of a dramatic procession through portals, with various reminders of nature suggested by a pergola. The outside environment was suggested by windows, and the colourful fabric was suggested not only by the samples of real cloth, but the polychromy of the walls. This *'architecture of suggestion',* a key to Graves' development of Post-Modern Classicism, was worked out at small scale before it was to be tried at large. Just as his kitchens and backyards were a testing ground for the

Sunar Furniture Showrooms in New York, 1979; Chicago, 1980; Houston, 1981; Dallas 1982. The portal, the framed entrance to a space, sets the major themes in colour and mood, while providing a monumental transition in space. Exteriors and landscape are evoked in these necessarily claustrophobic interiors cut off, as they are, from all contact with the outside. Simple classical themes, and abstracted elements such as the exaggerated architrave, are painted in many shades of what came to be known as the 'Graves palette'. This has influenced furniture and fabric as well as clothes. (Photo: Charles McGrath)

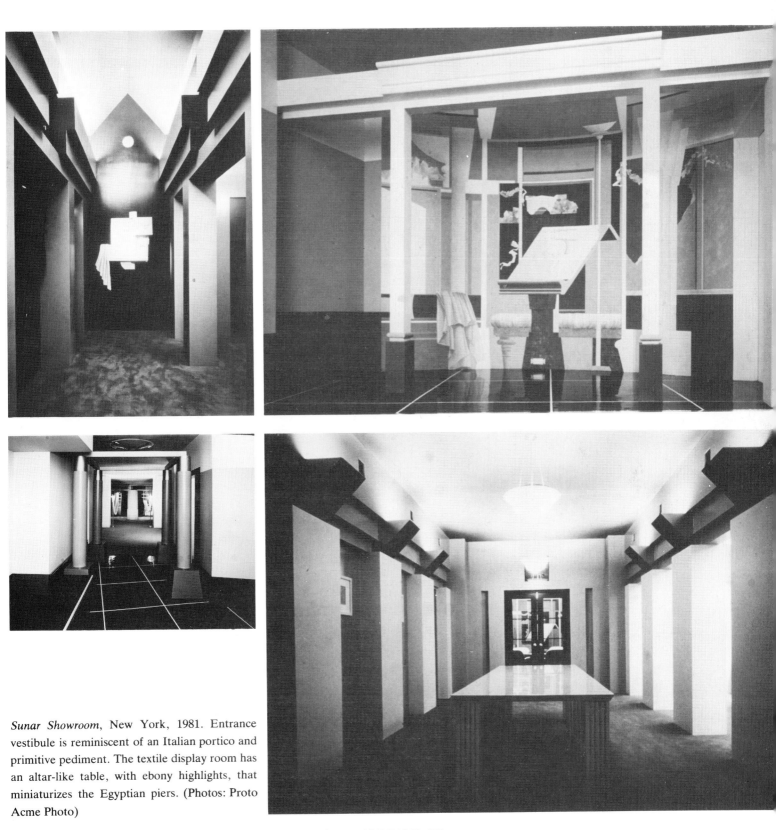

Sunar Showroom, New York, 1981. Entrance vestibule is reminiscent of an Italian portico and primitive pediment. The textile display room has an altar-like table, with ebony highlights, that miniaturizes the Egyptian piers. (Photos: Proto Acme Photo)

Sunar Showroom, Los Angeles, 1980. Measured, classical spaces of various shapes are organised on a processional route that has one culmination in the sculptural collage. Something like thirty-five shades of colour are used to define these various shapes: the predominant mood is Egyptian. (Top photo: Tim Street-Porter)

earlier Cubism, so now the furniture showrooms allowed him to experiment with a language at a price and size he could grasp. The Renaissance architect, such as Inigo Jones or Philibert de l'Orme, used stage scenery to work out architectural ideas, and Sunar served the same purpose for Graves.

Some of the experiments were rather heavy dead-ends. The early columns with their lumpish base and diminutive gold capitals had an undeniable freshness about them, but their proportions were Edwardian and pompous. The cheap constructional methods, using cardboard to imitate masonry, also produced a rather flat, bloated appearance in some of the details.

The Los Angeles Showroom has, characteristically, both the advantages and faults of other showrooms. One progresses on an enigmatic route, past the first, heavy Egyptian portal with its dark blue sky and sparkling, gold stars. Is the blue meant to symbolise the initiation into Sunar's mysteries? Or is it just an ironic comment on the 'Blue Whale', the building which houses this and other furniture companies?

Fabric cases, lined up like laboratory specimens, but under a gold pyramid, provide the first answer: this is an equation of mythic passage with commercial setting. Outside, swags of cloth hanging over golden balls are an indication to the public of what is sold. Yet it's more than an advertisement. The paradox is that commerce is given a dignity, swathes of cloth a grandeur, they usually never have. As the architectural promenade continues, past Cretan columns and primitive capitals, various memories are evoked of Egypt—the mysteries of embalming and sending the Pharoah's body on its continual journey into after-life. Then there is another clue, the Graves' collage with its signs of fabric, its archetypal house, green earth and coffee-pot. Here the good things of life are being offered up as the ritual objects which might be buried with the Pharoah. When we reach this first culmination under a dark sky, and pass through the next space, an Egyptian hypostyle hall, we assume the final room will be a climax to this carefully constructed plot. But it all ends in a room displaying modern furniture systems! The opportunities for ritual, which Graves is demanding in his architecture, would seem to be rather truncated by commercial reality.

Nonetheless in this and the New York Sunar Showroom, there are implications for a mythic monumentality right in the heart of consumer society. Static, hieratic shapes define a procession that is controlled and seemingly eternal. The transient nature of commerce, the business turnover of $55 million per year which Sunar is now making, is belied by the thick piers, proportioned to those of an Egyptian, funerary temple. Tables are elegant altars with incised lines picked out in ebony. End walls are voided pediments, a room is an extruded, coloured truss. All the meanings try to turn the evanescent materials into timeless icons and root commerce in a more dignified setting than it normally has. For the Late-Modern open-planning, the image and spur to change, it substitutes the Post-Modern answer of stasis and permanence: or at least their image.

A recent theme of Graves has been the necessity for returning myth and ritual to modern society, especially in the design of the house. We spoke of Wright's Ennis House as having a ritualised setting for family life organised around the altar-like dining table and adjacent hearth. Graves compared the thick piers of this house to his interest in the thick wall, and contrasted this with the usual insubstantial quality of Modern architecture.

CJ: Another parallel with Wright's work is the emphasis on the hearth. You've emphasised the fireplace by surrounding it with paintings of figures, caryatids, and angels.

MG: That's true. I've used the hearth as one of the places where the ritual of gathering can take place—with water, fire and other natural elements. The architect has a chance to play here with ideas of myth and ritual of the culture. Wright would place an inglenook to either side of a fireplace, and centre it in the room, whereas Le Corbusier would put it, almost, in the corner. He was asking us to be the New Twentieth-Century Man, as if we didn't need the hearth any more.

CJ: Wright often accompanied his fireplace with a written homily.

MG: The printed word is probably *not* of our time, because it expresses a singular, heroic idea. The allegorical painting, however, allows several thoughts to exist, simultaneously, with the idea of the hearth.

CJ: What are you trying to express in the paintings next to the hearth?

MG: The ritual of fire, the life of the occupants all coming together, the gathering of the family: it can be around a fire, or table, or window, or whatever is the most potent element in the room.

CJ: But your women seem to be offering something to the fire, in an almost religious sense.

MG: They're goddesses of the fire, both encouraging and dousing the flames.

A certain sad irony seems to accompany some of these wistful and beautiful altars. They seem to be stelae to a lost centre, to the family life and its sacred permanence that cannot be obtained in our society. The drawings of these icons have a melancholic air, the blues and terra-cottas and wispy outlines convey a lost dream.

During the period of Graves' involvement with Sunar, he fell in love with Linda Thompson, an attractive girl from California, who was an

Crooks House, fireplace, 1976. Rock and earth, fire and air, water and women—a diptych to either side of the flue. Like Wright's hearth at the Barnsdall House it's a ritual celebration of basic elements. (Photo: Graves)

executive also working with the company.[46] Their relationship, a stormy one for three years, almost ended in marriage: Graves nearly had, like Wright, the reality which his hearths, and monumental icons, symbolised. But the tensions, the jealousies between public and private, the marriage to a demanding profession which wanted all his time—again these proved too much.

✱✱✱

Venice Biennale on Post-Modern architecture, 1980. Post-Modern Classicism was the majority approach in this return to a street and facade architecture. Graves' construction is second to the left. The influence of Leon Krier can be seen in the vernacular work of this time.

1980 WAS THE YEAR THAT THINGS FINALLY STARTED TO GO RIGHT. IN January Graves won the competition for the Portland Public Services Building; in February he became involved in a public controversy over the building; in March he won another competition for the same building, vindicating himself and his public supporters, and through all this process he rose to become the public architect he remains. After eighteen years locked in the kitchen, the ghetto of the architectural 'compound', as Tom Wolfe calls it, he finally got out. Very few other architects live to escape.

In July of the same year Graves took part in the Venice Biennale, the first large-scale exhibition on Post-Modern architecture, and the event which, like the Weissenhof exhibition of 1927, announced a new, shared style. This international exhibit, organised by Paolo Portoghesi and other critics including myself, showed how varied Post-Modern Classicism could be: there was Bofill's transformation of Palladian grammar into giant mass-production; Venturi's and Stern's Commercial Classicism; Krier's and Purini's evocative Fundamentalist Classicism; Moore and Gordon Smith's Baroque Classicism; and then Graves' synthetic version which combined many of these strands[47]. One could identify a new international style here, only different from the one of fifty years before in being more hybrid and pluralistic. It was practised, by the architect, along with the other approaches, to be used, most fittingly on public buildings. Back were all the things which Modernism had thrown out during its 'vacuum cleaning period'. In a sense architecture had returned to its Pre-Modernist past, the eclectic mixture of historicist styles and modern technology. It was this eclecticism that Philip Johnson had attacked fifty years ago, in his book written in 1932 with Henry-Russell Hitchcock, *The International Style.*

CJ: Philip, you referred to Frank Lloyd Wright once as the greatest architect of the nineteenth century. What did you have in mind?

Philip Johnson: Well, it was perfectly clear that forty years ago Frank Lloyd Wright seemed like a very old character that was of no use any more to our International Style orthodoxy, and therefore he belonged to another era, in the nineteenth century. I wanted him out of the way, I didn't want him in any sense being a *Modern* architect.

CJ: But don't you regret that today?

PJ: Oh no! That was a perfectly good thing in its own context. I revere that man more than anybody except Richardson today.

CJ: You do?

PJ: Yes, in American architecture.

CJ: But he was using ornament, symbolism, polychromy—all the things you banished.

PJ: All the things we now look up to . . .

CJ: There's a connection between the present situation in architecture and the 1910s, don't you think?

PJ: I hadn't thought of that. I happen to love Coxhead and Lutyens, but I don't think of periods. I think of Palladio as much as I think of Lutyens.

CJ: I was thinking of people like Josef Hoffmann and Otto Wagner.

PJ: I think Josef Hoffmann is a very, very good architect. But one looks at him because so much is being published around him today. So it's like a new gift to see his Palais Stoclet, but I knew him and found him one of the most boring men I ever met. However, Lars Sonck is a new enthusiasm of mine. I'm not sure if he's any good or not, but I happen to be borrowing something from one of his towers right now. But, so what?

CJ: Well, because Lars Sonck was very interested in symbolism and that's an interest today.

PJ: One of *your* interests—I didn't know it.

MG: But Charles, you are partly right in one thing, which I hate to admit. We have eyes that look at certain people at certain times, that are more appealing to us than others. Philip went to Italy and came back with visions of Vittone, right? If he saw Vittone today he wouldn't be interested, as he'd be in C. F. Hansen or Peter Speeth, or somebody like that, where the symbolism is cranked up a bit.

CJ: Other architects being looked at are the generation of 1800, like Ledoux.

MG: Well, I have been criticised for that recently by Robert Venturi and others, for looking at Ledoux. But we look at *all* good architects, at everybody. It doesn't mean we copy, but we are influenced.

PJ: I am pure Ledoux. But I think I knew Ledoux before Michael did, simply because I'm older. I have just finished a building in Hawaii that's a dead ringer. I can't remember the exact page in Ledoux . . .

It's so much in the blood and it carries up through the German romantics and comes up through Schinkel.

CJ: I would say that both of your work has something in common with the larger tradition of classicism—what I call Free-Style Classicism.[48] Ledoux is characteristic because he took classicism in a very free way and created new moves in that chess game.

PJ: 'Contaminated Classicism'. I love that phrase of Peter Eisenman's.

From a purist point of view Michael Graves' classicism *is* contaminated. Like that of Leon Krier, it is related to the vernacular, or rather the idea of a basic *European* vernacular. Two schemes, finishing in 1983, show this. The public library, in San Juan Capistrano, makes partial use of the Spanish Mission Style, a manner required by a local

C. N. Ledoux, *House of the Directors of the Loue River*, Chaux, c1800. Free Style Classicism, a manipulation of the arch, podium, steps and Palladian motif in a new way to symbolise new functions. In this case the river flows through the building: compare it to the Fargo—Moorhead project of Graves, where the 'water' spilling from the scupper is in masonry!

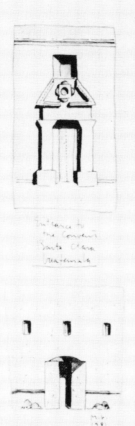

Public Library, San Juan Capistrano, referential sketches, 1980.

ordinance. We can recognise the stucco wall, wooden beams with stencil ornament and pantiles: they are all from this vernacular. But Graves has given these elements certain free style twists in his derivations: it is not 'borrowing' in Philip Johnson's phrase above, but closer to what T. S. Eliot meant by 'stealing'. 'The bad poet borrows, the good poet steals'. The old elements are transformed so the thief can get away with it. For instance, Graves has looked at Hispanic architecture in South America and re-derived the 'light monitor' from it. Here many little cupolas hover over the spine and allow the strong light to define interior points of interest. Graves' control of light in this dark library could be very pleasant since it filters in from many sources, most notably the monitors and arcaded courtyard. The drawings convey a Shinkelesque vernacular, the Italian farm buildings of that eclectic architect, which were often used in a palatial manner. So they are here, as well.

Public Library, San Juan Capistrano, 1981-3. A courtyard with four cypresses, is surrounded by a vernacular classicism made from gazeboes of trelliswork, stucco walls, wood beams, small windows and light monitors. Cream sides and ruddy pantiles set the background for figural shapes, water and red bougainvillia. (Photos: Proto Acme Photo)

Environmental Education Center, Jersey City, New Jersey 1980-3. A wildlife center opens out chapels off a central spine to view flora and fauna. The pyramidal massing focuses on the mythical small house or 'aedicule', extruded along the roof. The entrance pergola, when it is covered with growth, will accentuate the contrast of nature and culture. Primitive cedar siding, metal roofs and white stucco are the vernacular which is accented by classical columns and capitals. The wooden truss and pier are treated with an emblematic significance.(Photos: Proto Acme Photo)

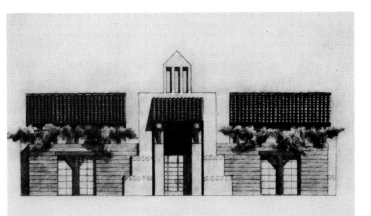

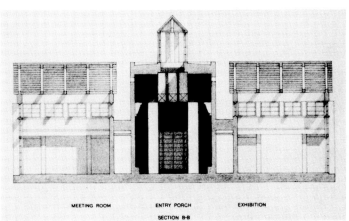

MEETING ROOM   ENTRY PORCH   EXHIBITION

SECTION B-B

Environmental Education Center, elevation and section. (Photos: Graves)

Even more part of the Italian vernacular is the Environmental Education Centre, or what Graves calls, less pompously, the Frog Museum. It is dedicated to the display and discovery of local wildlife: the flora, fauna and frogs which inhabit the New Jersey swamps overlooking the Statue of Liberty. Some of the materials used are part of the local vernacular—the roof forms and cedar siding—while other motifs are slightly Italian. Most obvious is the heroic wooden pier, with its outstretched arms, that both Graves and Krier have borrowed from Cesare Cesariano and any number of Lombardy barns.

But the complex is built in the best Yankee tradition of cheap wooden construction. The stud wall, the inexpensive framing and finishing techniques lend themselves to exploitation by a few individuals using small, power tools. A method learned at the Sunar Showrooms is that of using new materials which can be made to resemble the masonry ones of the past, specifically stone, which entailed specialist hand labour. With prefabricated sonar tubes, normally used for pouring concrete, with polymers and epoxies, fibreboard and 'spray-on terrazzo' (a quick painting method), one can represent an older expensive material with a mass-produced one.

The Frog Museum has a primitive freshness, like the Free Style Classicisms of previous periods, before they became academic. The bridge-like truss, the entrance arch, has a cool nobility, the cross between a flattened engineering structure and a monumental pediment. The village of chapels, which break out from the central spine to views of nature, are fundamental temples. The pillared approach, like Wright's Ennis House, cuts up light into a steady drum beat, the equivalent of the measured procession through yet another Egyptian funerary temple. In several such equations—barn with temple, vernacular with classical—Graves is showing the continuity in culture and buildings, from low to high, prose to poetry, vulgar and cheap to refined and luxurious.

THE BUILDING WHICH REALLY ESTABLISHED POST-MODERN Classicism, and Graves' reputation, was of course 'The Portland Building', as it has come to be known. This building has received such wide publicity that some of the story behind it is well known. But it still bears recounting in certain detail for the light it sheds on Modernist reactions to Post-Modernism.

Graves and his office, along with designers from the pragmatic office that specialises in skyscrapers, Emery Roth, produced designs in late December 1979 for a competition sponsored by the City of Portland, Oregon. It was a rare 'design and build' competition with a contractor submitting detailed cost-estimates along with the designs. Eleven competitors were reduced to a final three, in January 1980— the Arthur Erickson team and those of Mitchell/Giurgola and Michael Graves. All three had classicising elements, but the former two were Late-Modernist in their abstraction and use of high-tech imagery. They were also above the budget unlike the 'decorated shed' of Graves: a building that was the cheapest because the floors were squashed into the most economic, lumpish shape. In spite of the 'cosmetic frills', which of course lessened the heaviness, the real frills were in the other two schemes: their exaggeration of technology and spatial voids. Graves won the initial competition in January because of budgetary considerations—a cost of $22 million—and the strong recommendation of 'two jurors from the East Coast', Philip Johnson and his partner John Burgee. The presence and influence of these two annoyed local architects. A characteristic reaction, published in the local Oregon newspaper, brought out the paranoia.

> I can only conjecture that the citizens jury of five was duped into its decision. I have a feeling that the two Easterners, Philip Johnson and Graves, are chuckling in their beards over their achievement out west.[49]

But Graves and Johnson claim it was budgetary decisions which proved the most important factor, and reports from the committee would bear this out. Although Johnson did support Graves' entry into the final three, the ultimate decision came with an independent report of the City Council, submitted on February, 29, 1980, and this, while influenced by Johnson, lays stress on the cost.

CJ: Can you tell us how Michael won the competition.

PJ: Very simple. The upcoming major, Francis Ivancie, wanted someone to pick a scheme, and thinking I was reasonably objective— which I certainly was—I picked all three. And it was perfectly clear as we opened the submissions that only one spoke of genius—and that it came in on budget was just one of those lucky things that happens in this world.

Philip and the First Eight, 1980.
(Photo: Squire Haskins)

The outcry from local architects, something like sixteen from the Portland Chapter of the AIA, was supported by their spokesman, the Elder Statesman of Modernism, Pietro Belluschi. He made an address to the City Council, after its second report, on behalf of the FAIA, and characterised the building in churlish terms, which the Modernists had already used. They had called it a 'dog of a building', a 'turkey' (presumably for its squat, colourful shape) and ridiculed its 'pigeon coop' on the roof. Belluschi termed it 'an enlarged juke box' (again its square front?), an 'oversized beribboned Christmas package' that would soon 'be out of date'. He advised that it should be built, instead, in Atlantic City or Las Vegas. He charitably invited Graves to come 'live a little while among us and absorb the genius of our city', an irony not lost to Graves who pointed out that this invitation was written on his Boston stationery!

Belluschi, like SOM and so many Late-Modern multi-city offices, had ripped apart the centre of Portland with his glass and steel abstractions—denying the old fabric of cast-iron arcades and street architecture—and then he, like the others, had the gall to denounce Graves for being out of context. Well of course they were partially right. He didn't fit in, altogether, with their gridded boxes, by now the major convention in all cities. The ironies of this situation can be detected in the following exchange with Graves.

CJ: You had to win not only once but twice?

MG: We did—the second competition was between just two of us.

Temple design choice prompts debate

By STEVE JENNING
of The Oregonian staff

Local architects and Portland City Council members squared off in spirited debate Wednesday over the proposed temple design for the city's $32 million public service office building.

Submitted by architect Michael Graves and approved by a special jury that evaluated several competing designs, the plan was called a "dog building, a turkey" by one of nearly a dozen architects testifying at a City Council meeting.

Supporters responded, however, that the proposal's innovative nature was bound to draw criticism from traditionalist quarters. One said the building "'will in time be recognized as an important piece of art."

City Commissioner Mike Lindberg said he could not support Graves' design when the council votes next week on whether to enter final negotiations with the architect.

"In my opinion, the Graves' building is totally unacceptable," Lindberg said. "It's a fortress. It says government is monolithic, imposing and remote."

Commissioner Mildred Schwab responded that the council should not impose its collective "aesthetic values" on the design-selection process.

"If we do, I think we ought to throw the whole thing out and start over again," she said.

The stormy session began with salvos by Pietro Belluschi, a nationally known Portland architect, who argued that the council should not lean heavily on advice from its architectural consultant, New York-based Philip Johnson. Johnson and Belluschi both have received gold medals from the prestigious American Institute of Architects.

Johnson recommended the Graves proposal over two other submissions, which ran along more familiar glass and concrete lines.

"He (Johnson) is very witty and brilliant, but he is by nature an iconoclast," Belluschi said, adding that Graves' design might be better suited to Las Vegas or Atlantic City.

Belluschi also signed a letter submitted to the council from the local AIA chapter which condemned Graves' building facade as "trendy, almost cartoonlike."

"Architects and others with professional training are more likely to consider it as a laughingstock pervaded on our urban community," the letter said, alluding to the columns, masonry garlands and rooftop pavilions that adorn the building.

Architect James Jones said the council should formally poll local architects on the design for the 15-story, 412,000 square-foot structure that would be built on a city block between Southwest Main and Madison streets, and Fourth and Fifth avenues.

Miss Schwab criticized opponents for their timing. Since the designs were made public several weeks before the citizens jury selected a winner, Miss Schwab asked why opponents had waited until now to voice their complaints.

Architect Willard Martin supported the Graves design. Commenting on opposition, Martin drew a parallel with an attempt 20 years ago by some Portland residents to "outlaw" purchase of what they called modern art" for public projects.

"They (innovative artists) are the brave and the driven and the totally committed," Martin said.

Robert Frasca, another local architect and designer of the controversial Portland General Electric Co. headquarters — Willamette Center — argued that Graves is a "serious and talented architect" and called his design "distinguished."

"It's a good building, it's colorful where modern buildings are considered bland," Frasca said.

William Roberts, chairman of the design jury, said the council took "some risk" in accepting the competitive selection process.

"We were supposed to come up with a design that was to break the norm of (architecture) in the city," Roberts said. "If you wanted a mundane building, we would have come up with . . . different teams."

Roberts said the council "can't please everybody."

Lindberg said he supported a design submitted by architect Arthur Erickson, which provides a large public plaza facing Lownsdale Square. Data submitted Wednesday indicated annual maintenance costs for the two buildings are almost the same.

Sacrifice

EXCESS FRILLS DOO-DADS GADGETS

SOOTHING THE WRATH OF PELE

PORTLAND

TEMPLE-STYLE PUBLIC OFFICE BUILDING CONTROVERSY

Keep tradition

To the Editor: It is difficult to understand the aesthetics, the sense of history or those carping critics who have slandered Portland's proposed new temple of bureaucracy. Every precious little embellishment of this obscene baroque orgy is a tribute to the most stupefying works of government.

Is it merely gross, like the Victor Emmanuel monument in Rome? Can it suffer by comparison with the works of Ramses II, the ziggurats of Babylon or the new Senate office building in Washington? Or the Kremlin?

No, it comprehends the wondrous features of them all, in the cheapest possible form.

Psychiatry and architecture have always competed in the definition of mental disorders. This rivalry becomes visible in public buildings as megalomaniac masonry, and I personally fail to see why our City Council should be hindered in its faithful adherence to tradition.

LAMAR TOOZE,
801 Standard Plaza,
1100 S.W. Sixth Ave.

Design model?

To the Editor: Please note the following two pictures. The first is a model of Michael Graves' design for the new city office building.

The second picture is of a sage-hen grouse in full strut. The picture appeared in the February issue of Oregon Wildlife. The spread tail, cuffing feathers and puffed-up air sacs are important visual parts of the big show.

Could this be the Northwest inspiration for the Michael Graves design?

ELIZABETH JONES,
4145 S.W. Agate Lane.

Art historian finds Graves' plans compromised

By ANDY ROCCHIA
Journal Arts Writer

Except for its "Portlandia" sculpture, the city's new office building is almost complete and still the locals hardly know what to make of it.

However, Neil Levine has relatively few qualms. He loves it.

He considers the multi-hued structure (dubbed "Fort Ivancie" by some wags) an architectural breakthrough. In town recently to mull the curious state of late 20th century architecture in a talk at Portland Art Museum, Levine labeled the current "post-modernist" wave in architecture more than a mere ripple.

"The Portland Office Building is an ambitious manifestation of the mode. It is both lively and dignified," said the art and architectural historian from Harvard University, adding that the building's architect, Michael Graves, is but one of a not-so-small band of architects who are gaining a wider acceptance for a brand of design much removed from the austerity of orthodox modern architecture.

"This new direction is toward an architecture that re-uses historical forms, accepts the possibility of ornament, and emphasizes the relationship of a building to its neighbors. It is not mannerist nor decadent," said the 43-year-old scholar whose recent critical writings have run the gamut from gothic cathedrals and 19th century French Beaux Arts buildings to tracts on Frank Lloyd Wright.

But Levine has some reservations about the Portland Building, the chief one being he wished that city fathers had opted for Graves' plan as originally proposed.

"I WOULD HAVE liked more actual three-dimensionality with respect to the building's exterior. The building now looks very flat. One of the problems is the heavy base. It is so massive and in Graves' original plans that massiveness was to have been played off against a roof treatment that included towers and other fanciful and 'airy' additions. Also, the original garlands would have been much more sculptural. Now, despite the subtle use of paint to create the illusion of a more sculptural look, the building is nearly all flat. That sculpture over the entrance should alleviate the effect somewhat," said Levine, whose interest in the post-modernists stems from an admiration of the careful synthesis of classical elements in the buildings designed in the 1950s by American architect Louis Kahn.

"Kahn loved ancient history. His buildings are evidence of what architecture was before the modern movement took hold and before the separation began."

"That divorce from the decorative, from the figurative and the symbolic that took place in architecture never occurred in painting and the other visual arts.

"In painting, the artist never gave up the traditions of the figure, but architects gave up representation. The amount of things today's architects have given up is to me the big problem. To understand what representation has meant in architecture is a tremendous issue. All the shapes of historical architecture are re-creations of the primitive hut. The dome, for example, is but an update on

the canopy or tent, a primitive, natural form. All such forms from the dome to the post and lintel are shapes the architect has learned. In Graves, there are other sources of inspiration such as the mountains, attesting to his involvement in that relationship between history and nature," said Levine, who laments that so many architects think of a building as having to solve problems of plumbing, lighting and space. "So many do not deal with those shapes that give meaning to architectural form and, consequently, they are not doing the whole job."

LEVINE ALSO LIKED the first and second floor areas designed by Graves.

"The meeting room has a serenity that reminds me of the original theater of Wright's Johnson's Wax Building in Wisconsin. All those continuous lines and continuous surfaces."

The two window-like reliefs at the west and east ends of the second floor intrigued him, too. He skirted the question as to the symbolic value of the aforesaid appendages, but liked them for their purely visual values. "At first, these 'windows' look three-dimensional, but if you go back to them they are fairly flat.

"Beautiful" was Levine's opinion of the building's foyer.

"To be honest, I cavil at some of the materials used in the foyer and in the public spaces on the second floor. I wish they could have been richer, that more funds had been allocated to finish. But the building gives us a sense of what we would like."

Levine's holds the Portland Building comes as "a critique of what contemporary American society has been doing to itself."

"There's been a winding down of the modern style of architecture. The modern movement has been cheapened

and many architects can't just go on living with its precepts. Today, we don't tend to think of architecture as offering critiques of society but all great architects such as Le Corbusier and Wright have always done that. There's a tragic element in great architecture and we don't think of most architects as being involved in tragedy."

Levine believes to experience a building one has to visit it and in the case of the Portland Building, a trek to the 14th and 15th levels is a must.

"At the top of the building I had the feeling of being on a mountain. The view on the west is obstructed, but the feeling of a great achievement is there. On the west side there is this obstruction and you see this idiocy and you need this to tell you some things about your community

"In other words, when you are up there, you do get a feeling of what a crowning achievement a building's top can be; you also feel yourself as an individual with a special relationship to the city."

The historian believes that certain current trends in art and architecture have more to do with "central authority" (its presence or lack thereof) than with the condition of the world economy.

"PEOPLE ARE YEARNING for a kind of building that stands for the future. For example, when the great cathedral at Chartres was built it was not built for the present but for all time. We live in a time in which most buildings have not been built for an ideal. Now, however, attempts are being made to build for such. It's a shame there are so few. It's like you now have one good suit and go around looking like a slob the rest of the day."

Levine had relatively little to say about the building's "Portlandia" sculpture, other than the structure much demands a symbolic work. No really effective symbolic works in a classical mode have come to his attention on recent post-modernist buildings.

"I've seen photos of the models for the commission. The sculpture of the kneeling goddess is rather gentle and human. The model that features a kind of 'Nike of Samothrace' is more monumental. Don't be discouraged. Artists can rise to the occasion. Look at the Statue of Liberty . . . It was created by Frederic Bartholdi who was not an artist of the first rank. Liberty's face leaves a lot to be desired. But the Statue of Liberty is a fabulous thing because of its scale and placement. You took a chance on your building so why not take a chance on your sculpture?"

As part of its series celebrating the formal opening of The Portland Building, Portland Art Museum will be host to a talk by Michael Graves on Aug. 10 at 8 p.m., in the museum's Swan Auditorium.

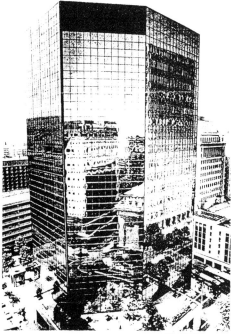

STEVE NEHL/*Oregon Journal*
NEIL LEVINE
'Look at the Statue of Liberty . . .'

BILL MURPHY/*Oregon Journal*
SO MUCH FOR THE VIEW — Architectural ideologies past and present meet head-on in mirror-like surface of Orbanco Building. Photo above was taken from 14th floor outdoor terrace of new Portland Office Building.

'Is Portland the birthplace of a new era of architecture?'

'Grow on' city

To the Editor: Architect Michael Graves' design for the city office building is certainly more interesting than the grey, characterless office towers that are rising everywhere.

It will be colorful and controversial, but it will grow on Portlanders, I think. It will certainly gain some nationwide attention.

MARTIN GIX,
017 S.W. Curry St.

Likes building plan

To the Editor: I was pleased to read of the citizens' panel's favorable response to architect Michael Graves' interesting and innovative design for Portland's new public office building.

As a downtown resident who is feeling increasingly boxed in by glass cubes and concrete monoliths, I look forward to a public building that offers more than the blank facades and mirror walls of modern architecture. As a taxpayer, I look forward to the savings

that Graves' building will make possible. His was the lowest bid.

The "temple" design shows more sensitivity to the design of neighboring buildings, the courthouse and City Hall, than its competitors. It is very likely more energy-efficient, and it gives Portlanders a building with visual interest for the first time in recent years.

PAUL MORRIS,
1834 S.W. Fifth Ave.

Portland Newspaper Clippings, 1980.

What happened is not clear to me to this day, but there was a political fight going on in town for the new mayor. One candidate was for our scheme, the incumbent mayor was for the other one.

CJ: The man who preferred your building was elected mayor?

MG: He was.

CJ: Are you saying that this building influenced politics?

MG: (grins) No, I wouldn't dare.

CJ: It certainly became a political building: you're surrounded here by buildings that are so different.

MG: Are they? Certainly the buildings that are built from the turn of the century up to 1940 are part of this language. The newer minimalist works are not, it's true. The new Portland doesn't fit into the one that was here.

CJ: Yet yours has black glass, uses abstraction, concrete and is a *partly* Modern building.

It makes allusions to the black, plate-glass building just to one side, and in several other senses repeats the abstract signs of Modernism. Thus although Modern buildings denied the old Portland, Graves hybrid Post-Modernism related to both new and old, the conflicting styles that were equally present. In this he was following the pluralist doctrine which is so essential to the new movement. The relation of Post-Modernism to the exclusivist Modernism has so far been one-sided: it might be called unrequited toleration.

That this is basically a political and public stance became clear as the controversy went on. Graves consciously designed a building that would engender different interpretations. The multiple meanings allow various groups to experience the building, instead of repressing their reactions the way monochromatic, and reticent governmental buildings do.

CJ: A lot of people are upset by the various imagery they see.

MG: I'm interested in the fact that the building is called *something*. Many of the other buildings here we can only call a box, in the pejorative sense of a shoe box. And we're lost, disoriented, because of that. If the detractors of my building call it a lot of names, and so do the adherents, at least they are identifying with it.

CJ: Many of the people of Portland supported you against the elite profession.

MG: That's true—the young people, the laymen, were very much in favour of the building. At least those who wrote letters to the editor and were interviewed in the street by the newspapers. The laymen seemed to be more open-minded than the local architects who were quite threatened by it. One thing that's happened since is that a number of people have approached me and said: 'you know, before

Portland Public Services Building, model, 1980. The epithet 'berriboned Christmas package' was obviously caused by the shape and flowing garlands. These were later turned to flat, stylised motifs so that the window cleaning equipment could pass. The building holds the street lines and relates to the tripartite structures to either side. (Photo: Princeton Photographics)

'Portlandia', over the entrance, signifies 'Port' with a trident, 'Land' with a sheaf of corn and trade with the East by a Chinese rock.

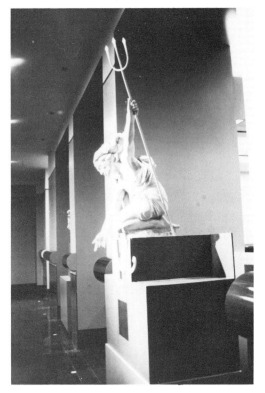

'Portlandia' sculpture by Raymond Kaskey, 1982, will be installed over the entrance.

your building we didn't care about architecture in this city. After your building we feel (whether we like it or not is not the point) we're part of the decision to make our city what it should be in terms of its architecture. We will require more of architects than we did before.'

So the *act* of architecture created the public realm and engendered a debate about some of the fundamental issues of meaning, cost and expression. Regardless of where one stood on the debate—Post-Modernism versus Modernism, temple versus understated box, decoration versus abstraction, modest cost versus high-tech luxury, East Coast versus West—the intervention of an architectural act started the forum by which it could be judged. The *res publica* which is usually housed in a building, can sometimes be momentarily created by a building. 'To build' is a verb and to build a public monument, which the 'Portland *Public* Services Building' must be, should involve some action on the part of the citizens. It may be, as the case here, demanding the return of certain sculptural and symbolic features: Belluschi and the Modernists had censored the figure of 'Portlandia', the citizens wanted it back. It may be cutting costs, adding new rooms, changing functions, or influencing style. All of these public events occurred, some of them disfiguring the building's top—where the pavilions and cantilevered platform don't exist—others improving the design. The ribboned garlands—for Graves a sign of Roman welcome and Christmas wreath—have been flattened, stylised and given the illusion of depth through *trompe l'oeil*. This was partly at the mayor's suggestion, the necessity for window washing equipment to move freely, and also a response to public reaction. Graves considers their more sober and stylised illusion an improvement. On balance the limited participation helped *and* hurt the design, but it undoubtedly catalysed public opinion on architecture, thereby raising consciousness about the environment. And it allowed the citizens to regard the building as partly their own. They are thus bound to look after it in the future.

As finally built, in the relatively quick time span from September 1980 to October 1982, this symbol of Post-Modernism has some obvious virtues and flaws. On the positive side it continues the street architecture of the old Portland, brings its dark, classical arcades up-to-date with green-tiled walkways. One critic of Post-Modernism, Kenneth Frampton, has faulted the building because it doesn't connect its public internal space with the park to the south, and allow movement through the heart of the building.[50] Where a grand doorway might have been, there is merely a suppressed parking garage. While this critique has a degree of truth, it overlooks the perfectly adequate arcade connections to one side. Another similarly

motivated historian, Kurt Forster, damns the building for its unpre-possessing interior space 'of crammed proportions', and then he goes on to criticise it for being at once too abstract and concrete: planar like flat Modernism and signs on a billboard. 'It is an almost gaudy package with ribbons, stick-ons, pop-ups, bows and strings, all neatly tied together with the pictorial greetings from an architect for all ideologi-cal seasons'.[51] This rhetorical criticism is perhaps a truer critique of the model than the final building, which is relatively free of attached elements. In any case the layered, symbolic quality can be seen as a positive virtue.

Undeniably the building is not a skyscraper, but a 'skylump'. Its economy is achieved by extruding the plot lines of the site upwards, repeating the sandwich office floor and keeping as low as possible. This lumpish quality is counteracted in three distinct ways: by the twin, vertical pilasters which represent the internal elevator cores; by the flare of the 'keystone' on the top four storeys, and by the change of materials and colour. All these devices, like classical *trompe l'oeil* techniques at Pompeii, idealise a rather pathetic reality: maximum economic exploitation. A Modernist committed to telling the truth no

Portland Building. The stylised garlands give the illusion of recession in a very small space of eight inches. The swag is a conventional sign of wel-come to a garden; here they reinforce the notion of the classical temple in the landscape.

matter how banal, might have expressed the lumpy reality in all its brutality; the straight classicist, believing in representing an ideal state, might dress the building as a white temple in Greek robes. Graves has done something in-between. He's combined idealism and realism. The concrete reality is expressed in its black window voids and pour-joints, but these elements are painted white and ordered to remind us of the ideal of rustication: the 'public' side of rustic building. The building's tripartite expression, like that of the human body—legs, torso and head—is of course a classicist conceit, but one which actually corresponds nicely with the building's different functions. The public realm and auditorium are at the foot, the similar office floors are in the longer torso, and the mechanical equipment and tetrastyle viewing pavilion are on the head. Also the 'faces' of the building, implicit metaphors which look out north and south through the 'eyes' of the flaring 'sconces', give it an undeniable classical reference, but one grounded in representation. Thus the classicism is very present, but *realistically grounded*, recalled but not copied. This has led to one of the strongest, and most intemperate attacks, that mounted by Wolf von Eckhardt in *Time* Magazine.[52]

In his broadside called 'A Pied Pier in Hobbit Land', Eckhardt seeks to discredit the building, and Post-Modernism, through a combination of innuendo, functional criticism and amusing abuse. Attacking others for brandishing labels, he lets off a veritable broadside of style-tags: 'heavy handed Pop surrealism' is the most prominent label, but Mickey Mouse Classical, rubbery ET and Sarastro's Temple of Isis are other epithetical contenders. As previously mentioned Graves' strong imagery elicits strong and sometimes wild reactions. And, it would seem, the distortions of classicism provoke some of the deepest feelings.

CJ: The temple and the face are classical images—different from Wright's imagery for government at Marin.

MG: His was a horizontal, this is a vertical building. The classical idea, if I can warp the question, concerns the notion of classification. Here the language separates and classifies the words 'door' as distinct from 'window', 'threshold' of the room as distinct from 'centre', 'ground' of the building as different from 'sky', the top.

CJ: So although it's a classical building in terms of its classifications, it's not a classical *revival* building.

MG: Yes, it's a Modern building which uses the classifications of the *language* of architecture—classical in its broadest sense.

CJ: A peculiar kind of classicism, a hybrid 'Modern Classicism'?

MG: Yes, or a 'Slang Classicism'.

The same sort of questions put to Philip Johnson elicited similar if

The north entrance 'face' has twin pilasters which represent the interior elevator cores. The black glass denotes the collective public realm, while the small windows represent each office floor and the energy crisis. Green tile at the base signifies the collective functions.

Plan of the first floor. The central spine connects the entrance lobby with the elevator core and the café to the rear. A covered arcade runs around three-quarters of the block, protection against the heavy rainfall of Portland.

The relation of building to street lines and adjacent classical buildings has been thought through. A general tripartite morphology has been kept, as indeed has the old Portland tradition of the covered passageway.

The interior of the central elevator bank has wide Torus mouldings used as a dado, and abstract classical elements which are back-lit and dramatised. The photo was taken before the furnishings were added.

more exaggerated replies.

CJ: Some critics hate it, calling the building 'Mickey Mouse Classical'.

PJ: Oh, that's good—that's a compliment. Peter Eisenman has an even better phrase—'Contaminated Classicism'. That's what I think our great aim should be—to so contaminate classicism that it won't be classicism. Or it will be classicism, but it won't be watered-down, thirties Paul Kleeism, or the emasculated work one sometimes sees today. Michael Graves is *so* strong in his shapes, *so* sure of his capitals and his keystones. His ornament is the most original that I know of. He has a way of utilising an overfat column, or the negative of a keystone, or using a keystone as a column. He can take things out of context and still make them beautifully balanced and classical . . . The big contribution of the Portland Building is the breaking through of the anti-Modern propaganda which Robert Stern and you have been fighting so valiantly for. And I've been doing my little bit. But of course I'm tarred with the Classical brush, more than the Post-Modern one.'

So Johnson, always the perceptive critic, implies the distinction between his own more revivalist work and that of Graves, crediting him with an originality that may be, from one viewpoint 'contaminated', but from another deeply creative. Originality within a language has always been the goal of Western classicism. One could argue, quite convincingly, that Graves' classicism is closer to 'imitation' than 'copying', nearer the *spirit* of tradition than the revivalist work of some of his contemporaries. In this sense then his work is a continuation of Wright's early period. A few critics are ready to place him in this tradition and among such august company, even if they might not make the parallel with Wright proposed here.[53]

The Humana Building, Louisville, Kentucky, 1982-5. A twenty-seven storey tower and block arrangement with a top 'head' and bottom giant door. The Secessionist grid, a Hoffman motif, tames the variety of colours and shapes. The Constructivist, cantilevered lookout seems fitting even though it's outside the normal classical language.

That Graves is a master of original composition can not be doubted, especially when one looks at his Humana Building, now under construction in Louisville, Kentucky. This, another competition winner, and against stronger competition—Cesar Pelli, Helmut Jahn and Norman Foster among others—will be a more vigorous building than Portland, because the budget is more than twice as big, and the censors are not allowed to strip off the ornament. More subtle colouring, real material and sculptural boldness will be obvious gains.

Partly the grammar is similar. Here are the same small square windows, tiny pavilions, giant doors and Roman cross-bracing. It's all done in Gravesian terra-cottas, blue pastels and ruddy accents. But the picturesque massing is more assured, the topmost barrel-vault turns easily into a truncated pyramid and that shape then swells out into a

Philibert de L'Orme, *Chapel at Chateau of Anet*, 1560. Pyramid, tempietto, curved pediments, chimneys and central planned volume are set in counterpoint.

curving balcony and culminates nicely in a central pavilion supported strangely by a Constructivist truss. The mixing of heterogeneous geometrical elements is masterful and in its accomplished vigour recalls the Free Style Classicism of Philibert de L'Orme. His Chapel at Anet also holds classical elements together while dramatising their opposition. The emphasis on simple volumetric expression is similar. Each one is adept at playing the intriguing game of 'disharmonious harmony'; only Graves incorporates a few disharmonious *materials*—notably the steel truss to play it with greater, twentieth-century tension. The presence of Cubism can still be felt even if it is now tamed within the integrating tendencies of classicism.

✳✳✳

Tea Service for Alessi, Milan, 1980. The monumental teapot. (Photo: Graves)

AS MICHAEL GRAVES APPROACHES HIS FIFTIETH YEAR HIS architecture has reached complete maturity. One can criticize it for not being technologically and socially radical, or fault it for being overly colourful and perhaps too 'contaminated', but these criticisms ultimately become carping: for Graves has given us something we didn't have before and the gift more than makes up for the failures. It may not excuse them, but we have to see them in context: the Pantheon is, as critics have observed for centuries, a dismally squat lump from the outside, more squat than the Larkin Building. The Taj Mahal and Villa Rotunda are virtually 'useless' buildings. All architecture has blemishes, especially when looked at from an unsympathetic angle. Graves' work is no exception and so it will, and should, be subject to criticism. But it has accomplished quite a bit as an art and its effects have been, on the whole, liberating. Concurrent with other architecture—notably that of Hans Hollein, Ricardo Bofill and the American Post-Modernists—it has opened up a monumental style which is

Joffrey Ballet production of 'Fire', sets and costumes by Michael Graves, 1982. (Photo: Graves)

accessible and free from cliché: popular without being populist. The style has been applied by Graves to designs for the Joffrey ballet, to tea and coffee sets as well as furniture. Style is not a substitute for content, but through conventional patterns it allows that content to exist publicly. It is the *sine qua non* of the public realm; without it we remain dumb, separate, incommunicative. The last great attempt to establish such a *lingua franca*, the International Style, was made on too narrow a spectrum. Post-Modern Classicism, I believe, is a wide synthesis which makes use of the full arsenal of architecture. Whether or not it will be accepted by society and really develop to maturity remains a question to be answered in 1990. If it does the reason will be that current architects, like the Pre-Modernists, tied it to vital technical and social facts. We are only taking the first step in the Post-Modern tradition, a beginning where art, ornament and symbolism are starting again. It is a rude beginning, like the Renaissance at its start, but just as fresh with discovery, hope and possibility.

NOTES

1   Le Corbusier, *La Ville Radieuse*, Paris 1933, as translated by Pamela Knight, Eleanor Levieux and Derek Coltman, as *The Radiant City*, Orion Press, New York/Faber and Faber, London, 1967, p. 60 ff.

2   *Moderna* was used positively in an architectural context by Filarete in the 1460s and has persisted with such connotations since then. See my *The Language of Post-Modern Architecture*, Academy Editions, London/Rizzoli New York, 1981, pp. 7-8, for references.

3   Frank Lloyd Wright, *An Autobiography*, Quartet Books, London, 1977, first edition 1932, p. 60.

4   For some of these influences see H. Allen Brooks' interesting article 'Frank Lloyd Wright—Towards a Maturity of Style 1887-1893', in *AA Files 2*, Architectural Association, London, July 1982, pp. 44-49.

5   For this interpretation see the fascinating article by Thomas Beeby, 'The Song of Taliesin' published Chicago, 1981.

6   *An Autobiography*, *op. cit.*, note 3, p. 159.

7   For this idea see Robert C. Twombly, *Frank Lloyd Wright, His Life and His Architecture*, John Wiley and Sons, New York, Chichester, Brisbane, Toronto, 1979, pp. 25, 32-57.

8   Rudolf Wittkower, *Art and Architecture in Italy, 1600-1750*, Harmondsworth, 1958, 1973 edition, p. 369.

9   John Lloyd Wright, *My Father Who Is On Earth*, G. P. Putnam & Sons, New York, 1946.

10   Frank Lloyd Wright, 'A Home in a Prairie Town', *The Ladies Home Journal*, February 1901.

11   *Ibid.*

12   Frank Lloyd Wright, 'The New Larkin Administration Building', *The Larkin Idea*, company publication, Buffalo, 1906. Excerpts in the perceptive review by Jack Quinan, 'Frank Lloyd Wright's Reply to Russell Sturgis', *Journal of the Society of Architectural Historians*, October 1982, p. 238.

13   *Ibid.*, p. 239.

14   *Ibid.*, p. 240.

15   *Ibid.*, p. 242.

16   *An Autobiography*, *op. cit.*, p. 175.

17   *Ibid.*, pp. 178-9.

18   'In the Cause of Architecture', *The Architectural Record*, March 1908.

19   Letter to Harriet Monroe, circa April 18, 1907, in the Monroe Poetry Collection, University of Chicago Library. I'm indebted to Joseph Connors for sending me a copy of this letter.

20   *Ibid.*

21   *Ibid.*

22   *An Autobiography*, *op. cit.*, pp. 186-7.

23   Margaret Allen, 'Family Memories of Four Sisters', published by Writers Workshop Books, Bombay, India, 1976, p. 25. A photocopy of this was kindly supplied to me by Thomas Beeby; unfortunately the full source was not identified.

24   *An Autobiography*, *op. cit.*, p. 187.

25   Quoted from Twombly, *op. cit*, note 7, p. 140.

26   NBC interview, 'A Conversation' with Hugh Downs, 1953.

27   *An Autobiography*, *op. cit.*, pp. 200-208.

28   See note 7; the story is told as 'A Regular Life is Cunningly Ambushed', pp. 173-210.

29   *An Autobiograpy*, *op. cit.*, p. 285.

30   *Ibid.*, p. 535.

31   *Ibid.*, pp. 248-256.

32   See Neil Levine, 'Landscape into Architecture, Frank Lloyd Wright's Hollyhock House and the Romance of Southern California', *AA Files 3*, January 1983, pp. 22-41, particularly page 36. Levine offers very suggestive insights in this article but does not necessarily support my own arguments for an anthropomorphic interpretation of the ornament and fireplace.

33 See Twombly, *op. cit.*, note 7, p. 229; Stephen Alexander, 'Frank Lloyd Wright's Utopia', *The New Masses*, June 18, 1935, p. 28.

34 NBC film, 'A Conversation' with Hugh Downs, 1953.

35 Remarks made at the time and quoted in *An American Architecture; Frank Lloyd Wright*, Horizon Press, New York, 1955.

36 For the concept of *difficultà* see John Shearman, *Mannerism*, Harmondsworth, 1967, pp. 21 and 41.

37 *Michael Graves*, Architectural Monographs 5, Academy Editions, London/Rizzoli, New York, 1979, p. 36.

38 The Synderman House has been quite extensively published, and can be found in the monograph, note 37, or in *Michael Graves, Buildings and Projects, 1966-81*, Rizzoli, New York, 1982/The Architectural Press, London, 1983.

39 Graves has said that Charles Moore's review of his work as being inaccessible made an impression on him, especially since it was from another architect acquainted with historial reference. See Charles Moore, 'In Similar States of Undress', *The Architectural Forum*, Vol. 138, May 1973.

40 *Op. cit.*, note 37, p. 52.

41 The blue balustrade as a lying column became quite an ironic point of contention between us; see my *The Language of Post-Modern Architecture*, 1977, *op. cit.* note 2, pp. 64 and 66.

42 Graves wrote a blurb for the back flap of the 2nd edition of *LPMA* describing it as favouring an 'accessible language'. His work had been moving in this direction since the Crooks House of 1966, but didn't synthesize conventional elements into a stable whole until the Plocek House of December 1977-March 1978.

43 The International Style was called 'Le Style Corbu' for some time before 1925. While Gropius and others synthesized it in part in 1911, it took a painter, furniture designer and urbanist to give a convincing visual synthesis.

44 *Op. cit.*, note 37, p. 82.

45 Robert Venturi has raised the question of his early Post-Modern Classicism in 'Diversity, relevance and representation in historicism, or plus ça change . . .' *Architectural Record*, Vol. 170, June 1982, pp. 114-119. While Graves has indubitably learned from Venturi, he's also synthesized many other influences to produce an amalgamation uniquely his own.

46 Linda Thompson is an executive with Sunar, head of the textile division, and a very attractive woman; see Richard K. Rein, 'In The Race to Challenge "Glass Boxes" Architect Michael Graves is Building a Solid Lead', *People*, February 1982, pp. 87-8.

47 The 1980 Venice Biennale has been published in many magazines and a catalogue: *The Presence of the Past*, Rizzoli, New York/Academy Editions, London/Electa, Milan, edited by a team led by Paolo Portoghesi.

48 See my 'Free-Style Classicism: The Wider Tradition', *Architectural Design* Profile, Academy Editions, London/St. Martin's Press, New York, 1982.

49 See a letter to *The Oregonian*, quoted in my 'Post-Modern Classicism' *Architectural Design*, 5/6, 1980, p. 138.

50 Kenneth Frampton has made these points in an RIBA Annual Discourse, December 1982, and the *LA Architect*, January 1982.

51 Kurt W. Forster, 'The Building', *Skyline*, January 1983, pp. 16-18. This *Skyline* collects interesting opinions on the work.

52 Wolf von Eckhardt, 'A Pied Piper in Hobbit Land', *Time*, August 23, 1982, pp. 62-3.

53 Vincent Scully in the monograph, note 38, or *Skyline*, note 51, places him in the company of the masters; Paul Goldberger notes his importance in 'Architecture of a Different Color', *New York Times Magazine*, October 10, 1982, pp. 41-66; I have been writing about it since 'Post-Modern Classicism', *Architectural Design*, 5/6 June, 1980. Obviously many books will soon challenge, and some confirm, this view.